MW00578681

OUR FATHER, WHO ART IN HEAVEN

OUR FATHER, WHO ART IN HEAVEN

UNDERSTANDING *the* SIGNIFICANCE *of* THE LORD'S PRAYER

WILLIAM H. WETMORE

AUTHOR OF *HIM WE PROCLAIM*

© 2010 by William Wetmore. All rights reserved.

Pleasant Word (a division of WinePress Publishing, PO Box 428, Enumclaw, WA 98022) functions only as book publisher. As such, the ultimate design, content, editorial accuracy, and views expressed or implied in this work are those of the author.

No part of this publication may be reproduced, stored in a retrieval system, or transmitted in any way by any means—electronic, mechanical, photocopy, recording, or otherwise—without the prior permission of the copyright holder, except as provided by USA copyright law.

Unless otherwise noted, all Scriptures are taken from the *Holy Bible, New International Version*®, NIV®. Copyright © 1973, 1978, 1984 by the International Bible Society. Used by permission of Zondervan. All rights reserved.

Scripture references marked KJV are taken from the *King James Version* of the Bible.

Scripture references marked NKJV are taken from the *New King James Version*, © 1979, 1980, 1982 by Thomas Nelson, Inc., Publishers. Used by permission.

Scripture references marked RSV are taken from the *Revised Standard Version* of the Bible, copyright 1952 [2nd edition, 1971] by the Division of Christian Education of the National Council of the Churches of Christ in the United States of America. Used by permission. All rights reserved.

ISBN 13: 978-1-4141-1734-8
ISBN 10: 1-4141-1734-5
Library of Congress Catalog Card Number: 2010902670

THE TWO VERSIONS OF THE LORD'S PRAYER

MATTHEW AND LUKE (KING JAMES TRANSLATION)

After this manner therefore pray ye: Our Father who art in heaven, Hallowed be thy name. Thy kingdom come, Thy will be done in earth, as it is in heaven. Give us this day our daily bread. And forgive us our debts, as we forgive our debtors. And lead us not into temptation, but deliver us from evil: For thine is the kingdom, and the power, and the glory, for ever. Amen.

(Matt. 6:9-13)

And it came to pass, that, as he was praying in a certain place, when he ceased, one of his disciples said unto him, Lord, teach us to pray, as John also taught his disciples. And he said unto them, When ye pray, say, Our Father who art in heaven, Hallowed be thy name. Thy kingdom come. Thy will be done, as in heaven, so in earth. Give us day by day our daily bread. And forgive us our sins; for we also forgive every one that is indebted to us. And lead us not into temptation; but deliver us from evil.

(Luke 11:1-4)

CONTENTS

PREFACE
OUR FATHER WHO ART
IN HEAVEN

The Spirit himself testifies with our spirit that we are God's children.

(Rom. 8:16)

Love your enemies and pray for those who persecute you, that you may be sons of your Father in heaven.

(Matt. 5:44-45)

And he [Jesus Christ] told them a parable, to the effect that they ought always to pray and not lose heart.

(Luke 18:1-2 RSV)

Come to me, all you who are weary and burdened, and I will give you rest. Take my yoke upon you and learn from me, for I am gentle and humble in heart, and you will find rest for your souls. For my yoke is easy and my burden is light.

(Matt. 11:28-30)

THE LORD'S PRAYER has always had a certain fascination for me. The reason is that it represents the summary of the basic teaching on prayer that Jesus Christ has given to His disciples to be used in every age. His disciples came to Him and said, "*Lord, teach us to pray.*" When His disciples asked Jesus to teach them to pray,

Jesus answered with this great prayer, recorded in Matthew and Luke. Above all, Jesus told us to pray to *Our Father* in this manner.

This prayer makes holiness attractive. It unites us to our heavenly Father. It contains most of the great doctrines of Christianity. It is simple in its appeal. It is profound in its meaning and teaching. It is a prayer that I have said thousands of times. However, it is a prayer that I have never fully understood nor said with the conviction that it deserves. It is a prayer we have repeated so often that we can say it without thinking. We can murmur the words and miss the truths proclaimed in this prayer.

Anyone can say the words. However, it can only have true meaning to the children of God, the redeemed of the Lord, the born again, and God's children who can call God, *Our Father.*

The promise of Scripture is that God hears and answers our prayers, in the power of the Holy Spirit. The miracle is this: God joins us in prayer, and we have a divine conversation leading to a divine relationship. As a result, we experience the joy and the power of prayer.

Jesus said that we are always to pray and never give up. He further said, *"Come to me and I will give you rest,"* and, *"Learn from me."* What we are to learn is how prayer is instrumental in developing our eternal relationship with God. And so we have this wonderful prayer. It is simple in content, but powerful in appeal and meaning.

Is it a powerful prayer? Without a doubt! Does the prayer speak to the thoughts of God? Without a doubt! Does it proclaim the truths by which our lives are to be directed? Without a doubt! Therefore, I have decided to study these great Christian doctrines of our faith in order to understand the convictions I am expressing in *The Lord's Prayer.* In addition, deep down inside this prayer, Jesus calls us to see the glory, the power, and the majesty of God.

There is also a series of Discussion Questions at the end of each chapter to emphasize the principal issues and significant points covered in that chapter. Such questions may be useful for individual and group Bible Study.

I want to thank my dear wife, Nancy, for her encouragement and helpfulness in the editing and preparation of this book. She has blessed me greatly.

"Lord, I pray: help me; teach me—to speak this prayer with truthfulness, honesty, conviction, faithfulness, and in a manner that truly honors and shows reverence for all that You are and all that You have called us to be."

—**William H. Wetmore**

THE LORD'S PRAYER

CHAPTER 1

WHEN YOU PRAY...PRAYER: AN OVERALL PERSPECTIVE

Rejoice always, pray constantly, give thanks in all circumstances; for this is the will of God in Christ Jesus for you.

(1 Thess. 5:16-18 RSV)

May the God of peace, who through the blood of the eternal covenant brought back from the dead our Lord Jesus, that great Shepherd of the sheep, equip you with everything good for doing his will, and may he work in us what is pleasing to him, through Jesus Christ, to whom be glory for ever and ever. Amen.

(Heb. 13:20-21)

THE SUBJECT OF this book is The Lord's Prayer—its purpose, meaning, significance, importance, and power in and for our lives. However, before addressing the substance of that prayer, I believe it is important to examine several specific subjects relating to prayer in general. In doing so, I believe this will provide a good foundation for the study of The Lord's Prayer.

Let me begin by stating my previous view of prayer. Prayer was not important to me in the past. Prayer to me had no real power. However, I have since learned some valuable lessons that have given new meaning regarding prayer in general and The Lord's Prayer in particular. Jesus told His disciples, *in this manner*, you are to pray.

1

This short prayer points to the power and majesty of God, the dependence of man on God, and God's eternal will for His creation.

Among many truths, we are told to delight in the Lord (see Psalm 37:4). This we can do through prayer. Also, God wants us to honor Him, not with our lips, but in our hearts (see Matthew 15:7-9). This we can do through prayer. Further, God wants us to worship Him in spirit and in truth (see John 4:24). This we can do through prayer.

God has proclaimed, through His apostle Paul, that we are to rejoice always, pray without ceasing, and give thanks in all circumstances (see 1 Thessalonians 5:16-17). The joy of the Lord, His peace, and our thanksgiving are all united in prayer. God wants to equip us with everything good for doing His will (see Hebrews 13:20-21); this we can do through prayer.

I often wonder: how can I acknowledge that God is omnipresent, omnipotent, and omniscient and yet fail to pray to God in every situation and circumstance in my life? Since He is all that Scripture proclaims, He can and will move to advance His kingdom, as well as meet the needs of His children. For me, prayer is the greatest opportunity for fellowship and relationship with God. My prayers are no longer a casual event.

This self-examination has led me to recognize six important truths: 1. Prayer is a divine conversation. 2. Jesus Christ is both teacher and example in prayer. 3. Prayer is important. 4. Prayer has power. 5. Our attitude and spirit in prayer are crucial. 6. We should pray with faith, trust, and high expectations.

PRAYER IS A DIVINE CONVERSATION

What do you think is the measure of any meaningful relationship? Suppose I told you I think honest, truthful, and respectful conversation is possibly the most important measure of our relationships. Now, if that is true, then there are at least four fundamental truths I've learned about conversations: 1. Conversations are a measure of our relationship. 2. Conversations mean dialogue. 3. Conversations involve an exchange of ideas, thoughts, feelings, etc.

4. Conversations are not about you or about me; conversations are meant to be about *us*.

On a human level, what would it mean if you never talked to your wife or your kids? What message would that send? What would that say about those relationships? When you have a conversation with your spouse, it speaks volumes about your relationship. Again, when you and your spouse don't talk, that also describes your relationship. When you and your kids don't talk, what does that tell you about your relationship? In general, I am convinced that conversation is essential to relationship. It's that simple. In general, people talk to people they like. People really want to talk to those they love.

Let's move now from human relationships to divine relationship, our relationship with God.

Honest, respectful, loving, and reverent conversation with God is what the Bible calls prayer. If you accept that definition of prayer, then let me move to my second question. It is one that only you can answer. So I ask you, in a divine sense, do you like God? Or better yet, do you love God?

Keep in mind that Jesus summarized the law in Mark 12:29-31. *"'The most important one,' answered Jesus, 'is this: "Hear, O Israel, the Lord our God, the Lord is one. Love the Lord your God with all your heart and with all your soul and with all your mind and with all your strength." The second is this: "Love your neighbor as yourself." There is no commandment greater than these.'"*

We are to welcome these two commandments because loving God implies that we spend a lot of time with God in prayer. In addition, we are to love our neighbor as we fulfill the second commandment. Prayer is one example of our love for God. Other examples that demonstrate our love for Him are studying and treasuring His Word, obeying His commands, serving Him, being His witnesses, and being His ambassadors for reconciliation.

Prayer, this divine conversation, is rooted in love. Jesus said that loving God is the key to the Christian life (see Mark 12:29-31). Love is giving and receiving. It is receiving love from God and from our neighbor. It is giving love to God and to our neighbors.

3

For God so loved the world that he gave his one and only Son, that whoever believes in him shall not perish but have eternal life.

(John 3:16)

I ask you, do you love God? Does your conversation reflect your love? In a divine sense, do you talk *to* God and do you talk *with* God? I used to talk *to* God; I never talked *with* God. There is a big difference.

If you don't talk to God, what does that tell you about your relationship with Him? It almost says, "*I don't like God. I surely don't love God.*" If you don't pray, that is an indication that you don't like God. It could surely mean that you don't love God, you don't know God, you don't believe in God, and you don't trust God. I believe the Bible teaches that prayer is a divine conversation that leads to a divine relationship.

The first important truth I have learned about prayer is that God knows all about me and my circumstances. I need to speak truthfully from my heart with God. Another important truth is that divine conversation is an exchange of thoughts and ideas. When we enter the presence of God to pray, we are there for an exchange. Therefore, before we pray, we first ought to be quiet and listen to what God has to say to us. There is every reason to believe that what God has to say to you and me is much more important than what we have to say to Him. Only after listening to God do we present our petitions. After that, we should listen quietly to see what response God might have. Prayer, this divine conversation, should begin and end by hearing what God has to say.

One fundamental truth about life is this: human beings were created to love and to be loved. Many people have discovered what the Bible has taught us for centuries—that without love, human life becomes empty and meaningless. It becomes spiritually, emotionally, mentally, and physically void. Only love can give meaning and purpose to life. Only our response to God's love can lead to eternal life. Love is the key. God has shown His love for us in the Cross. By the passion of Jesus Christ, God is saying how much He loves us, how much He wants to redeem us, how much

4

He wants us to be reconciled to Him, and how much He wants to give us eternal life.

But how can I show that I love God? What is the measure of my love? The Bible teaches that my obedience to Him, my trust, and my faith in Him are three clear examples of my love for God. Another important measure of my love for God is the content and depth of my prayers. I believe prayer leads to communion with God, which is a divine relationship with Him. Finally, fellowship and communion lead to divine unity. John 17 emphasizes this divine unity. *"That they may be one as we are one: I in them and you in me. May they be brought to complete unity to let the world know that you sent me and have loved them even as you have loved me"* *(John 17:22-23)*. I believe the Bible teaches that prayer is one of the essential bases for a loving and eternal relationship with God. I have come to realize that prayer is a divine conversation.

JESUS CHRIST IS BOTH TEACHER AND EXAMPLE IN PRAYER

It is interesting that Jesus Christ is called *teacher* by every element of Jewish culture—Pharisees, rulers, His apostles and disciples, Nicodemus, and Jews in general. More importantly, He identified Himself as our Teacher.

> *When he had finished washing their feet, he put on his clothes and returned to his place. "Do you understand what I have done for you?" he asked them. "You call me 'Teacher' and 'Lord,' and rightly so, for that is what I am. Now that I, your Lord and Teacher, have washed your feet, you also should wash one another's feet. I have set you an example that you should do as I have done for you. I tell you the truth, no servant is greater than his master, nor is a messenger greater than the one who sent him. Now that you know these things, you will be blessed if you do them.*
>
> (John 13:12-17)

The fact that He is Lord is the foundation of the fact that He is Teacher. As Lord, He has the authority and the power to teach with all wisdom and knowledge and truth. His truth and wisdom are indisputable. They are uniquely important in His teaching relating to prayer. Three passages, among many, reflect the teachings of Jesus on prayer.

> *But I tell you: Love your enemies and pray for those who persecute you, that you may be sons of your Father in heaven.*
>
> (Matt. 5:44-45)

> *Therefore I tell you, whatever you ask for in prayer, believe that you have received it, and it will be yours.*
>
> (Mark 11:24)

> *So I say to you: Ask and it will be given to you; seek and you will find; knock and the door will be opened to you. For everyone who asks receives; he who seeks finds; and to him who knocks, the door will be opened.*
>
> (Luke 11:9-10)

Jesus told us to be bold and confident people; we are to ask, seek, and knock. Jesus promised that when we do, whatever we ask shall be given, whatever we seek we shall find, and whatever we knock upon shall be opened to us.

The Christian world has acknowledged Jesus Christ as a teacher. They believe the title He claimed for Himself. The question is: do we acknowledge Him as Teacher?

Christ's disciples came to their Teacher and asked Him to teach them to pray. Think about it. Why did they do that? They could have asked Him to teach them many things, but they asked Him to teach them to pray. Why didn't they ask Him to teach them to heal or to teach or to cast out demons or anything else they had seen Him do? Rather, they asked, *"Lord, teach us to pray."* We too must listen to the Teacher; we must see the Example of the Teacher; we must behold the glory of the Teacher.

PRAYER IS IMPORTANT

I told you that prayer is important, but why is it important and what is the evidence of its importance? The Bible teaches us that prayer is important for at least four reasons.

First, God said that His house was to be a house of prayer (see Isaiah 56:7 and Matthew 21:13). If prayer is important to God, it has to be important to me.

Second, Jesus Christ was the everlasting witness to the importance of prayer. Jesus prayed before every significant act in His earthly ministry. Above all, He prayed as He prepared for the Cross. John 17:1 and 2 begin with these words, "*After Jesus said this, he looked toward heaven and prayed: 'Father, the time has come. Glorify your Son, that your Son may glorify you.'*" The life of Jesus was a life of constant and unceasing prayer.

Third, the Patriarchs were men of prayer. To them prayer was vital to their very existence. Abraham prayed to God (see Genesis 20:17), Isaac prayed to God (see Genesis 25:21), Moses prayed to God (see Exodus 8:30), Manoah prayed to God (see Judges 13:8), Samson prayed to God (see Judges 16:28), Hannah prayed to God (see 1 Samuel 1:10), Samuel prayed to God (see 1 Samuel 8:6), Saul prayed to God (see 1 Samuel 14:41), David prayed to God (see 2 Samuel 15:31), Elijah prayed to God (see 1 Kings 18:36), Elisha prayed to God (see 2 Kings 6:17), Hezekiah prayed to God (see 2 Kings 19:15), Ezra prayed to God (see Ezra 9:5-6), Daniel prayed to God (see Daniel 9:4), and Jonah prayed to God (see Jonah 2:10). To the patriarchs, prayer was as important as breathing. One lives by breathing; Christians live by prayer. If it was important to all the Old Testament patriarchs, prophets, and kings, it must be important to me. It was equally important to the New Testament disciples.

Fourth, Jesus told His disciples: "*When you pray, say...*" (see Matthew 6:5). Again I repeat, Jesus did not say, "*if you pray*, but "*when.*" Prayer is important because it unites us with the God of all creation and all authority and power. In a personal and spiritual way, prayer unites us with our heavenly Father. It is divine conversation essential to a divine relationship. This divine relationship is with our God, who is omnipresent (ever present), omnipotent (all powerful), and omniscient (all knowing). He is all that and much more. He is love. He is grace and mercy. He is patient. He is kind. He is abundant in blessing. This is the God to whom we pray. This is the One who, in the fullness of His time, hears and answers our prayer. And that's why prayer is important.

From these passages, we learn that trust and faith are keys to receiving the promises of God. Other aspects of prayer are love, obedience, and service. Love leads to obedience; obedience leads to service. All three are important for receiving the gifts of God, the paramount of which is the gift of the Spirit.

Is prayer important? You bet it is. Consider all the reasons we have just discussed. God is the Reason. Fellowship is the Reason. Communion is the Reason. Hope in Eternal Life is the Reason.

Prayer's importance lies in its power, described throughout the Scriptures.

PRAYER HAS POWER

Prayer is important not only because of the divine conversation and divine relationship with God, but because God is omnipotent and there is great power in the prayers of a righteous person. *"The prayer of a righteous man is powerful and effective"* (James 5:16).

Let me summarize at least seven truths regarding power in prayer. First, God is near us whenever we pray to Him. *Come near to God and he will come near to you (see James 4:8)*. God is near His people who come near to Him; God is near the faithful nation. Deuteronomy 4:7 says, *"What other nation is so great as to have their gods near them the way the LORD our God is near us whenever we pray to him?"* What power! Second, if you believe, you will receive what you ask for in prayer. What power! Third, God gives us hope, riches, and His incomparable great power to those who believe. What power! Fourth, we are given the power to have the incomparable love of Christ and to be filled with the fullness of God. What power! Fifth, know that the good work He began in each of us, He will carry it on to completion. What power! Sixth, know that by His power, God will fulfill every good purpose for us and every act prompted by our faith. What power! Seventh, know that if we ask, we will receive. What power!

There is power in all of our relationships with God. One of the most important relationships occurs through prayer. Prayer has power because our omnipotent God is involved, and God is all powerful. Jesus knew prayer's power and prayed to His Father in power in every circumstance. He knew the Father, the source of power. He knew that God will give power to those who ask Him. But what is this power that we speak of? Let us look at what the Scripture teach us about this word, *power*.

We begin with the recognition that God is all-powerful and the source of all divine, spiritual, and physical power. He is the Omnipotent; His power is always good, and He uses it to accomplish His good purposes (1 Chronicles 29:11; Psalm 145:11; Revelation 7:12).

> *David praised the LORD in the presence of the whole assembly, saying, "Praise be to you, O LORD, God of our father Israel, from everlasting to everlasting. Yours, O LORD, is the greatness and the power and the glory and the majesty and the splendor, for everything in heaven and earth is yours. Yours, O LORD, is the kingdom; you are exalted as head over all."*
>
> (1 Chron. 29:10-11)

By His power, God has the ability or strength to perform any activity or deed that He desires. By His word and by His breath, God created the universe and everything in it. In the Bible, the word *power* relates to the presence of God. God is power, and the Spirit works through the people of God to give us the power essential to fulfill the work given to us by God. Along with power, God also gives us authority to use that power wisely and for His glory.

Associated with the word *power* is the word, *authority*. God has both the power and the authority to use power in the best interest of His plan for His creation and His kingdom. Listen to the evidence of the Old Testament.

> *Then Moses left Pharaoh and prayed to the LORD, and the LORD did what Moses asked.*
>
> (Exod. 8:30-31)

The LORD has heard my cry for mercy; the LORD accepts my prayer.
(Ps. 6:9)

O you who hear prayer, to you all men will come. When we were overwhelmed by sins, you forgave our transgressions.
(Ps. 65:2-3)

The LORD detests the sacrifice of the wicked, but the prayer of the upright pleases him.
(Prov. 15:8)

The LORD is far from the wicked but he hears the prayer of the righteous.
(Prov. 15:29)

The New Testament also witnesses to the power of God as revealed in His Son. As God incarnate, Jesus Christ had both power and authority (see Luke 4:36), and He has given much authority and power to His disciples (see Luke 10:19).

However, I am not only going to tell you that prayer has power, I am also going to prove it to you from the Word of God. Of the multitude of examples of the power of prayer in the Bible, I have selected fourteen as representative of God's hand and demonstrated power in the midst of His people. I encourage you to study each text in order to understand both the Presence and the Power of God in response to the prayers of His people. 1. The plagues preceding the Exodus (see Exodus 9:27-29). 2. The prayer of Hannah for a son (see 1 Samuel 1:10-17, 27-28). 3. In the wilderness, God answered prayers, given by Moses (see Numbers 21:4-9). 4. Elijah, in the power of God, confronts and defeats the priests of Baal (see 1 Kings 18:16-41). 5. Resuscitation of the physically dead (see 2 Kings 4:32-35). 6. A righteous king, Hezekiah, restores the glory of God in Judah (see 2 Kings 19:9-34). 7. God fulfills His promise, given in Joel 2:28, to send the Holy Spirit (see Acts 4:31-34). 8. God gives the Holy Spirit to those who ask (see Acts 8:15-17). 9. The prayers of the faithful lead to the resuscitation of the dead (see Acts 9:40-42). 10. God's promises to those who humble themselves, pray, seek His face, and turn from their wicked way that they will have their sins forgiven (see 2 Chronicles 7:14). 11. God will listen to those who pray to Him, when they seek Him with all their heart (see Jeremiah 29:12-14). 12. God answers the prayers of those who trust in Him (see 1 Chronicles 5:20-21). 13. The prayers of the church will be answered and lead to freeing the saints of God (see Acts 12:5-7). 14. The prayers of the righteous imprisoned were answered by God (see Acts 16:25-30).

These few examples demonstrate the power of God in response to the power of prayer. However, in our prayer life, we must have the right attitude and the right spirit.

OUR ATTITUDE AND SPIRIT IN PRAYER

Jesus taught his disciples to pray, but there is an *attitude* about prayer that must be understood and manifested. He said our attitude should include the following: a love that includes our enemies (see Matthew 5:44), an attitude that seeks the Will of God (see Matthew 26:36-39), an attitude of forgiveness of ourselves and others (see Mark 11:25), an attitude of faith and trust even before we begin to pray (see Matthew 21:22; Luke 22:32), an attitude that values the peace and joy of solitude in our prayers (see Matthew 14:23), an attitude that glories in communion with God (see Luke 6:12), an attitude of sincerity (see Luke 22:40-44), an attitude that seeks the Face of God (see John 17:1), an attitude of humility (see 2 Chronicles 7:14; Luke 18:10-14; James 4:6), and an attitude of righteousness (see Matthew 26:41).

Our attitude is critically important. I have learned that attitudes lead to actions, actions lead to habits, habits lead to character, and character leads to our final destiny. I want to have an attitude that leads to eternal life.

Jesus said we need not only the right attitude, but we must also have the right *spirit*. First, we must be in the power of the Spirit. Second, our heart must be right with God. The heart stands for the human center of our moral, spiritual, and intellectual life. Our hearts must first be pure so that our thoughts and our actions are pure and pleasing in the sight of God (see Psalm 15:1-3; Matthew 5:8;

11

Matthew 22:37). Third, we must have clean hands (see Psalm 24:4) and a clean heart (see Psalm 51:10). In Scripture, cleanliness refers to moral purity. Clean hands are a symbol of innocence, sanctification, and purity. Fourth, we must have a broken spirit and a contrite heart (see Psalm 51:17). Fifth, we must be *born again* (see John 1:12-14; John 3:3, 5). Sixth, we must be people of faith (see Mark 11:24). Seventh, we must have a forgiving spirit (see Mark 11:25). Eighth, we must ask in the name of Christ (see John 14:13-14).

To have a meaningful prayer relationship with our Father, the proper *attitude* and *spirit* must be present in our lives.

OUR EXPECTATIONS IN PRAYER

If we are truly people of prayer, the primary question is, "What are our expectations?" Do we go to prayer, expecting that God is present, that He cares for us and wants to hear our petitions? Do we believe God hears our prayers? Do we believe in a God who is omnipotent and has the power and the will to meet our needs as He deems appropriate and in our best interests? Do we believe that God wants to fulfill His purposes for our lives?

We should be bold and confident and expect great things to occur in prayer and after prayer. We should have that expectation even before we go into prayer. We should believe that great things will happen in the presence of a great God. Our expectations should be high. We should be confident that God will be who He says He will be. Trust Him. Have faith in Him. Expect the highest and the best.

Therefore I tell you, whatever you ask for in prayer, believe that you have received it, and it will be yours.

(Mark 11:24)

So I say to you: Ask and it will be given you; seek and you will find; knock and the door will be opened to you. For everyone who asks receives; and he who seeks finds; and to him who knocks, it will be opened.

(Luke 11:9-10)

Until now you have not asked for anything in my name. Ask and you will receive, and your joy will be complete.

(John 16:24)

We should have high expectations. Jesus said, believe that you have received it. Jesus said, we receive not because we ask not.

In conclusion, eight main ideas about prayer are developed. First, prayer is divine conversation and an expression of our love for God; second, divine conversation leads to a divine relationship; third, Christ is both our teacher and our example for a life of prayer; fourth, prayer is important because it unites us with our Father; fifth, prayer has power because the omnipotent God is involved; sixth, the proper attitude and spirit are essential for meaningful prayer; seventh, Scripture witnesses to the importance and power of prayer; eighth, we should have high expectations that God who hears our prayer has both the desire and the power to meet our petitions.

Discussion Questions

1. How does Hebrews 13:20-21 help you in your prayer life?

    _____

    _____

    _____

    _____

2. How did you previously view both the importance and the significance of prayer?

    _____

    _____

    _____

    _____

3. What should be your attitude in prayer?

    _____

    _____

    _____

    _____

4. What should be your spirit in prayer?

    _____

    _____

    _____

    _____

5. How do you view the importance of conversation to relationship?

_____

_____

_____

_____

6. What are some basic truths regarding conversation?

_____

_____

_____

_____

7. How do you think the Bible defines prayer?

_____

_____

_____

_____

8. How well do you believe that you fulfill the two great
   commandments?

_____

_____

_____

_____

9. What can you and should you do differently to fulfill them more completely?

_____

_____

_____

_____

10. Do you love God? How do you express that love?

_____

_____

_____

_____

11. Do you love your "neighbor"? How do you express that love?

_____

_____

_____

_____

12. Do you believe that prayer is divine conversation? Why do you believe that?

_____

_____

_____

_____

13. Do you consider Jesus Christ as your Lord and Teacher? How is that evident in your life?

_____

_____

_____

_____

14. How is He Lord to you? How is He Teacher to you? What does He teach you about prayer?

_____

_____

_____

_____

15. Is prayer important? Why?

_____

_____

_____

_____

16. Does prayer have power? In what ways?

_____

_____

_____

_____

17. What are your current expectations in prayer?

_____

_____

_____

_____

18. What should your expectations be?

_____

_____

_____

_____

CHAPTER 2

AFTER THIS
MANNER ... PRAY YE

After this manner therefore pray ye: Our Father who art in heaven,
Hallowed be thy name. Thy kingdom come. Thy will be done in earth,
as it is in heaven. Give us this day our daily bread. And forgive us
our debts, as we forgive our debtors. And lead us not into temptation,
but deliver us from evil: For thine is the kingdom, and the power,
and the glory, forever. Amen.

OF ALL THE prayers in Scripture, I have to believe that this is one of the most important. Why? Because this is the only prayer that Jesus taught His disciples that includes you and me. It is not a prayer that we should say casually. This prayer demands our utmost attention because it is a gift from the Son of God. I know I have said this prayer in the past without truly thinking about what I was saying. I know now that to say this prayer without understanding or conviction does not bring honor to God. Because I have said this prayer for so many years without fully meaning what I said, I have decided to do so no longer. I want what I speak to God to be from my heart. I trust His words. I want God to trust my words. I want to mean what I say to God.

So this book is really a journey, reflecting on much of what I have learned regarding the significance of The Lord's Prayer. The prayer is important and meaningful because it brings us face to face with many of the great doctrines of the Christian faith. Further, in this prayer, we turn to God to seek His provision, His pardon, and His protection. To begin, let me ask you a few questions.

Why did the disciples come to Jesus and ask Him to teach them to pray? Why does Jesus tell us to address God as our Father? What did John the Baptist teach his disciples about prayer that was so meaningful to the disciples of Jesus? What are the messages in this prayer? Why did Jesus tell us to pray in this manner? What lessons did He want us to learn as we pray in this manner? What meaning does this prayer have in my life? When I have finished praying, what do I think should happen? Why do we say this prayer at every service? Is it that important? In the remaining chapters, we shall discuss these and other significant questions.

One thing Jesus is telling us is this. God is eternally all in all. He is everything to us and for us. On the other hand, we are His dependent children whom He loves. In addition and by way of introduction, a discussion of the following areas will set the stage for a more definitive discussion of The Lord's Prayer.

IT HONORS AND ADDRESSES GOD AS FATHER

Jesus tells the disciples we should pray to the Father. We are not to pray to the Spirit; we are not to pray to the Son. However, prayer is trinitarian. We are to pray to the Father in the power of the Spirit (see Romans 8:26-27), and make petitions in the name of the Son (John 16:26).

IT ELEVATES OUR VISION FROM OUR WORLD TO GOD'S KINGDOM

Jesus wraps this prayer in the terms of His kingdom; we are to pray in kingdom-language. In the beginning, He instructs us to pray for the coming of the kingdom. At the end of the prayer, He tells us to acknowledge to God, the Father—thine is the kingdom.

IT ADDRESSES MANY OF THE GREAT DOCTRINES OF CHRISTIANITY

Notice how many of the great doctrines of Christianity are proclaimed in this prayer. We have the Fatherhood of God (see Chapter 3); the nature of heaven (see Chapter 4); the reverence and praise we ascribe to God (see Chapter 5); the names of God reflecting the person and character of God (see Chapter 5); the kingdom of God (see Chapter 6); the Will of God (see Chapter 7); the provision of God for His people (see Chapter 8); the nature of sin (see Chapter 9); the temptations of Satan (see Chapter 10); the person of Satan (see Chapter 11); the glory, power, and majesty of God (see Chapter 12); and finally, both God the Father and Jesus Christ, each the great amen (see Chapter 13).

IT ADDRESSES BOTH SPIRITUAL AND PHYSICAL PETITIONS

Jesus focuses our attention in prayer to three things: first, our need for *bread* (physical and spiritual); second, our need for *forgiveness*; third, our need for *protection from temptations and from the evil one (Satan)*.

Two other aspects of this prayer become obvious. First, it is a corporate prayer. Notice all the pronouns. They are all plural—*our, us*. Notice that the first word in the prayer is *our*. This is an extremely important point. We are not praying just for ourselves, we are praying for others who share similar concerns, needs, and the desire to glorify the Father. This is a prayer for the Body of Christ. Second, it is not a prayer for individuals. There is no way an individual can pray, *Our Father*. Jesus does not tell us to pray, *My Father*. However, the only thing we can say is that the prayer does offer a model that individuals can use effectively in their personal prayer life.

There are many classic books and teachings on this prayer. I am going to focus on one by Dr. Haddon Robinson and another by Dr. David Jeremiah.

First, Dr. Jeremiah in *Prayer, the Great Adventure* has devoted approximately half the book (Part Two) to a discussion of The Lord's Prayer (see Matthew 6:9-13 and Luke 11:2-4). Dr. Jeremiah's discussion of the Lord's Prayer is divided into the following main sections: *Praise*: Our Father, who are in heaven, Hallowed be Thy name; *Priorities*: Thy kingdom come, Thy will be done on earth, as it is in heaven; *Provision*: Give us this day our daily bread; *Personal Relationship*: Forgive us our debts as we forgive our debtors; *Protection*: Lead us not into temptation, but deliver us from evil; ending where we began: For thine is the kingdom, and the power, and the glory, Amen.

Second, in one of his teachings, Dr. Robinson has a similar structure, with slight variations. For example, he uses the following: *Person*: Our Father who art in heaven, Hallowed be thy name. Thy kingdom come. Thy will be done, as in heaven, so in earth; *Provision*: Give us day by day our daily bread; *Pardon*: And forgive us our debts (sins), as we forgive our debtors (those who sin against us); *Protection*: And lead us not into temptation; but deliver us from evil; *Person*: For thine is the kingdom and the power and the glory. Amen

Both outlines are very helpful and both have considerable merit; however, I have decided to use Dr. Robinson's format, with slight variations.

Finally, it is important to note that various translations may present this prayer with different words. For example, sometimes *Our Father* is translated as just *Father*; sometimes *Our Father, who art in heaven* is translated *Our Father, which art in heaven*. Sometimes *sin* is translated as *debt,* sometimes as *trespasses.* Sometimes *evil* is translated as *the evil one.* Finally, some translations do not include the phrase, *For thine is the kingdom and the power and the glory. Amen.* I will discuss these differences in the chapters that follow.

Let us now address two of the questions I raised at the beginning of this chapter. First, why does Jesus encourage us to pray in this manner? I admit it is difficult, perhaps impossible, to understand the mind and purpose of God. Saying that, I also believe God expects, and even encourages, His children to make a serious and conscientious effort to understand His deepest truths. With that understanding, I believe Jesus taught His disciples this prayer for three reasons.

First, Jesus wanted us to understand, appreciate, honor, and love God as our Father. Jesus proposes a new and closer relationship. God is enthroned in heaven, but now God has a closer relationship with His adopted children. As Creator of all, Jesus has now defined God as accessible to all. Since He is our Father, then that defines us as His children. Defining God also defines us.

> What other nation is so great as to have their gods near them the way the LORD our God is near us whenever we pray to him?
>
> (Deut. 4:7)

Second, Jesus knows that human beings have two fundamental needs: the physical and the spiritual, which can only be fully met by God, our Father.

Third, Scripture emphasizes that Jesus came to proclaim the kingdom of Heaven. He wants us to emphasize the kingdom in our daily lives. He wants us to be kingdom-directed people.

Moving now to the second question, is there a single thought or statement that would express the theme of this prayer? In other words, how would I explain to myself or anyone else what this prayer is all about? The single thought might well be this.

The God of all Creation, whom we are privileged to call our Father, whom we are to acknowledge and worship, calls us and invites us to recognize we are His children, we are to come to Him for every need (physical and spiritual), and we are to serve Him and advance His kingdom.

In the chapters that follow, we shall address the specifics of The Lord's Prayer.

Discussion Questions

1. Why do you consider the Lord's Prayer important?

_____

_____

_____

_____

2. What aspects of the prayer are important to you?

_____

_____

_____

_____

3. What is the significance of calling God "our Father"?

_____

_____

_____

_____

4. What great doctrines of the Christian faith are covered in this prayer?

_____

_____

_____

_____

5. Why did Jesus tell us to pray "in this manner"?

_____

_____

_____

_____

THE PERSON OF GOD

CHAPTER 3

OUR FATHER

HIS PERSON-1

*After this manner therefore pray ye: "**Our Father** who art in heaven, Hallowed be thy name. Thy kingdom come. Thy will be done in earth, as it is in heaven. Give us this day our daily bread. And forgive us our debts, as we forgive our debtors. And lead us not into temptation, but deliver us from evil: For thine is the kingdom, and the power, and the glory, forever." Amen."*

For if you live according to the sinful nature, you will die; but if by the Spirit you put to death the misdeeds of the body, you will live, because those who are led by the Spirit of God are sons of God. For you did not receive a spirit that makes you a slave again to fear, but you received the Spirit of sonship. And by him we cry, "Abba, Father." The Spirit himself testifies with our spirit that we are God's children. Now if we are children, then we are heirs — heirs of God and co-heirs with Christ, if indeed we share in his sufferings in order that we may also share in his glory.

(Rom. 8:13-17)

T HE TWO BASIC themes we shall address in this chapter are the fatherhood of God and the children of God. The first theme is that God, as our Father, has an eternal love and concern for His children. The second theme is that which relates to the children of God and has two dimensions. First, the present: the children of God are those who are led by the Spirit. Second, the future: the children of God will share in the glory of God.

It would follow that the children of God are those who have been born of the Spirit (see John 1:12-14; 3:3, 5) and have the indwelling Spirit within them (see 1 John 3:24). Being *led by the Spirit of God* would be impossible without the new birth and the indwelling of God's Spirit. I encourage you to keep those themes in mind as we address the person of God, which will be our focus for the next five chapters.

"Our Father who art in heaven, Hallowed be thy name. Thy kingdom come. Thy will be done in earth, as it is in heaven."

We begin this sequence by looking at the significance of *our Father*. The first truth that becomes apparent is this is a corporate prayer. United with fellow believers, we address the Father. By those two words, Jesus brings His disciples—you and me—into a union with God that the Son of God enjoys. He is our Father; we are His children. To claim God as Father means we express not just a relationship, but also a dependency and a willingness to obey His command and to seek His Will and do whatever He calls us to do. To acknowledge God as Father is to acknowledge His authority over our lives and His power in our lives. Our response to God as our Father is simply obedience, which is a positive and active response to what a person knows and hears. True obedience can be the greatest expression of love.

Our Father is the way in which Jesus directs us to address the God of the universe. The apostles speak of God as the Father of our Lord Jesus Christ (see 1 Peter 1:3; Ephesians 1:17). Although Christ taught His disciples to address God in prayer as *our Father*, He spoke of God as *my Father* and *your Father*. As Father, God is in a special sense the Father of His redeemed and reconciled people.

In the initial clause *our Father*, we express His nearness to us. In the latter phrase, *who art in heaven*, we express His distance from us. Both expressions are important in the divine relationship. The fatherly relationship of God to His people is evident throughout Scripture, beginning in the Old Testament.

*He [God] is the Rock, his works are perfect, and all his ways are just. A faithful God who does no wrong, upright and just is he. They have acted corruptly toward him; to their shame they are no longer his children, but a warped and crooked generation. Is this the way you repay the LORD, O foolish and unwise people? Is he not **your Father**, your Creator, who made you and formed you?*

(Deut. 32:4-6)

*But you [God] are **our Father**, though Abraham does not know us or Israel acknowledge us; you, O LORD, are our Father, our Redeemer from of old is your name.*

(Isa. 63:16)

*Have we not all **one Father**? Did not one God create us?*

(Mal. 2:10)

The Old Testament message is carried over into the New Testament. In fact, Jesus makes the fatherhood of God one of the central themes of His earthly ministry.

*In the same way, let your light shine before men, that they may see your good deeds and praise **your Father** in heaven.*

(Matt. 5:16)

*And do not call anyone on earth "father," for you have one **Father**, and he is in heaven.*

(Matt. 23:9)

He is the Father, who cares because He loves; and His love is a sign of His giving. He is a loving, giving God, as expressed in John 3:16 and 17, *"For God so loved the world that he gave his one and only Son, that whoever believes in him shall not perish but have eternal life. For God did not send his Son into the world to condemn the world, but to save the world through him."*

God loved; He gave, so that He could save. Herein is the great message that God's love was expressed in His giving His Son, for the singular purpose which was *"to save the world through him."*

31

But can everyone call God, *Father?* I think not. I believe that only the children of God can call God their Father. For example: on a human level who can call you father? Only those who have been born or raised by you can call you father. Can other children call you father? I think not. What is true for an earthly father is also true of God, our heavenly Father. God can only be the Father of those who are His children.

The question of relationship revolves around the issue of the nature of our birth. And the question is: what is the nature of our birth? Have we only been born physically with only a physical father? Or have we been born spiritually? Do we have both a physical father and a spiritual Father? You see, we can be the child of God for only one reason: because we have been born of the Spirit of God. That is the truth that Jesus told Nicodemus: you must be born again.

He [Jesus Christ] came to his own home, and his own people received him not. But to all who received him, who believed in his name, he gave power to become children of God; who were born, not of blood nor of the will of the flesh nor of the will of man, but of God.
(John 1:11-12 RSV)

As a result of a spiritual birth, God is our Father, and we, the *born again,* are His children. It is that simple; it is that profound.

But what does it mean for God to be our Father? The idea is one of paternal love and care. A father is the father of the needy, and children at all ages are needy. A father is also a teacher, with the idea of paternal instructions. The father is responsible for bringing up his children in the fear (awe and reverence) of the Lord, generally acting as their instructor and guide (see Exodus 12:26; Deuteronomy 6:20). Children are to honor their father, be obedient to their father, and they are not to rebel against the authority of their father. These characteristics are true of earthly fathers. How much more are they the characteristics and attributes of our heavenly Father!

Honor your father and your mother, so that you may live long in the land the LORD your God is giving you.

(Exod. 20:12; Matt. 15:4)

However, God is to be honored for He is the Father of the righteous, of kings, and priests, and prophets. Honor is due the earthly father (see Exodus 20:12; Matthew 15:4). Certainly God, as our spiritual Father, deserves and merits much more honor than that we would give to our earthly fathers. But there is another aspect of this relationship; God is not only our Father, but we, as His children, have a vision of the kingdom of God and we will share eternity in the kingdom of God.

Jesus answered him, "Truly, truly, [Amen, Amen] I say to you, unless one is born anew, he cannot **see the kingdom of God."** *Nicodemus said to him, "How can a man be born when he is old? Can he enter a second time into his mother's womb and be born?" Jesus answered, "Truly, truly, I say to you, unless one is born of water and the Spirit, he cannot* **enter the kingdom of God."**

(John 3:3-5 RSV)

There is only one way we can see and enter the kingdom of God—by the new birth, the spiritual birth. We must be *"born again"* to be a child in God's kingdom.

The Gospel is the message, adoption through propitiation, that we have become the adoptive children of God, through the cross of Jesus Christ, through the propitiation of Christ (see 1 John 2:1-2), through our confession and repentance (see Romans 10:9), and through our faith (see Ephesians 2:8-10).

So, Jesus says, when you pray, begin by addressing God as *"Our Father."*

This is the first step in examining the Person of God. The second step is to consider what Jesus meant us to understand when He directed us to pray: *Who art in heaven.*

Discussion Questions

1. What does it mean to call God our Father?

_____

_____

_____

_____

2. What does it mean to use the possessive "our"?

_____

_____

_____

_____

3. What do you learn from the following passages?
   a. Deuteronomy 32:4-6

_____

_____

_____

_____

   b. Isaiah 63:16

_____

_____

_____

_____

c. Malachi 2:19

_____

_____

_____

_____

d. Matthew 5:16

_____

_____

_____

_____

e. Matthew 23:9

_____

_____

_____

_____

4. What does John 3:16 tell you about the fatherhood of God?

_____

_____

_____

_____

5. Can anyone address God as our Father?

_____

_____

6. What qualifications must you have to address God as our Father?

7. How does calling God our Father relate to the kingdom of God?

CHAPTER 4

WHO ART IN HEAVEN
HIS PERSON-2

*After this manner therefore pray ye: Our Father **who art in heaven**, hallowed be thy name. Thy kingdom come. Thy will be done in earth, as it is in heaven. Give us this day our daily bread. And forgive us our debts, as we forgive our debtors. And lead us not into temptation, but deliver us from evil: For thine is the kingdom, and the power, and the glory, forever. Amen.*

Now I know that the LORD saves his anointed; he answers him from his holy heaven with the saving power of his right hand.
                                                                (Ps. 20:6)

I lift up my eyes to the hills — where does my help come from? My help comes from the LORD, the Maker of heaven and earth.
                                                                (Ps. 121:1-2)

From that time on Jesus began to preach, "Repent, for the kingdom of heaven is near."
                                                                (Matt. 4:17)

WE NOW BEGIN to identify God not just as our Father, but as the One who is in heaven. That immediately raises several questions of the significance of God's presence in heaven. Where

37

is heaven? Where is God? What is the nature of heaven? Is heaven God's only dwelling place?

To address these and other questions, we will examine two significant subjects: first, the nature of heaven and earth; second, the reasons that Jesus came down to earth: His relationship to the concept of heaven.

In addition, as we address these two topics, we will examine specifically three terms: *heavens, heaven, and earth.* Understanding these subjects is essential to appreciating the fullness of *Our Father who art in heaven....* We will also begin to comprehend the character of the heaven that Jesus speaks of in Matthew 4:17.

It is important to recognize that this prayer deals with the concept of heaven twice: first, in this passage heaven indicates where God is; second, heaven is reflected in the petition that God's will be done in earth, as it is in heaven. In the prayer, notice that the singular form, heaven, is used.

THE NATURE OF HEAVEN AND EARTH

We need to understand heaven from the perspective of God, of Christ, of the Holy Spirit, of believers, of Satan, and of unbelievers. We shall touch on each of these perspectives in this section.

The Bible uses two words—one plural and the other singular: *heavens and heaven.* Heavens relates to the multiple heavens that God created. Many theologians consider that the Bible refers to as many as seven heavens. The third heaven is considered the holy place, the dwelling of God. Heaven may well be used in the Bible to denote this third heaven.

And what do the heavens do? *"The heavens declare the glory of God; the skies proclaim the work of his hands. Day after day they pour forth speech; night after night they display knowledge. There is no speech or language where their voice is not heard"* (Psalm 19:1-3).

Although the word, *heaven,* is used predominantly in the New Testament, it is first used in Genesis 14:18-19, *"Then Melchizedek king of Salem brought out bread and wine. He was priest of God Most High, and he blessed Abram, saying, 'Blessed be Abram by God Most*

*High, Creator of **heaven and earth**.'"* The last use is in Revelation 21:10-12, *"And he [an angel] carried me [John] away in the Spirit to a mountain great and high, and showed me the Holy City, Jerusalem, coming down out of **heaven from God**. It [the heaven] shone with the glory of God, and its brilliance was like that of a very precious jewel, like a jasper, clear as crystal."*

Is there any distinction or does heavens include heaven? I think the Bible teaches there is no distinction; as expected, heaven is part of the heavens. However, *heaven* is the dominant word used in this prayer. It is also the dominant word in the ministry of Christ and of His church. This prayer, then, focuses on that third heaven, and that will be the emphasis of our discussion.

In general, Scripture tells us heaven is everything that has authority and power over man, gods, and spirits. In that sense, heaven became a general expression for everything that has positive and meaningful power and authority over man. Heaven means *up*. Earth means *down*. Heaven conveys the thought of going up, such as climbing a mountain. It is up to the things of God and down to the things of man. That is not, however, an eternal condition.

Two words, *ascent* and *descent*, are closely associated with the concept of heaven. *Ascent* signifies pardon and life. *Descent* means condemnation and death. In His coming to earth, Christ bridged the gulf between heaven and earth and became man. He became like us, so that we could become like Him. At His baptism, when Jesus came up out of the water, it was the prelude to a specific action by God. With His elevation on the Cross, He ascends to where he was before (see John 6:62). His descent reveals the Father's love. His ascent confirms God's sovereign power. In His descent and ascent, He bridges the gulf between God and the world, between light and darkness. The ultimate purpose of God behind the ascent and descent is our growth in personal maturity in Christ.

With the symbolism of *ascent* and *descent*, *up* and *down*, there is the scriptural difference between *above* and *below*, between heaven as God's sphere and earth as man's. However, that is not necessarily an appropriate contrast because heaven and earth were both created by God and are both in His sphere. Although earth may be more fully man's sphere, in this age heaven definitely is not in man's sphere. Therefore, we have the distinction between a holy God and the sinful world. It is in this context that we can begin to understand the difference between heaven and earth. In summary, up goes to above; down goes to below.

When we consider heaven, the emphasis is not so much on God's *dwelling*, but on God's *presence* in His dealings, first with Israel, and then with all the nations. In 1 Kings 8:12-13, God is said to dwell in the temple. However, fifteen verses later in 1 Kings 8:27, Scripture says the whole of heaven could not contain God. These statements are not contradictory; they merely represent the progression in the view of God in heaven and on earth.

As the theology of Israel grew, an important understanding began to develop that Yahweh was now the God of heaven. This title became very popular (see Ezra 5:11; Daniel 2:18).

> He [Daniel] urged them to plead for mercy from the God of heaven concerning this mystery.
>
> (Dan. 2:18)

Not only was God the God of heaven, but He began to be recognized as enthroned in heaven (see Isaiah 6:3; Psalm 82:1; Daniel 7:9). Daniel, in about the sixth century BC, wrote, "*As I looked, thrones were set in place, and the Ancient of Days [God] took his seat. His clothing was as white as snow; the hair of his head was white like wool. His throne was flaming with fire, and its wheels were all ablaze*" (Daniel 7:9).

This new view of God as enthroned in heaven replaced the old view of the God of Sinai. Mankind began to get a higher vision of God in heaven. This progressive revelation of heaven now presents God, not only as enthroned in heaven, but also as the One who fills the earth with His glory. God is recognized as King and Lord Almighty. God reigns in glory in heaven. He likewise reigns in glory on the earth. We now begin to see a strong evidence of God, present both in heaven and on earth.

As the vision of God increased, the tendency to avoid the use of His name increased. Man began to substitute the word *heaven* for the name of God. Later even the word, *heaven,* was replaced with *Lord, Kyrio.* Progressive revelation of God continued in a very significant way. He began to reveal Himself, not only as God enthroned in heaven, but now more personally as our Father in heaven (see Matthew 5:16; 12:50). In Christ, God turns towards man. God now becomes the Father of all nations. It is interesting that the name assigned to Abram was Abraham, meaning *the father of many nations.* *"No longer will you be called Abram; your name will be Abraham, for I have made you a father of many nations" (Genesis 17:5).* In this regard, Abraham foreshadows the fatherhood of God, by God taking on the role as the Father of all nations.

As the view of God in heaven and earth progresses, so the view of heaven begins to take on an enlarged dimension. In agreement with the Old Testament, the New Testament reaffirmed the creation of the heavens and the earth by God (see Acts 4:24; Revelation 10:6) and that He will recreate them (see Isaiah 65:17-19; 2 Peter 3:13; Revelation 21:1). For many reasons, the present heaven will pass away like the earth (see Mark 13:31; Revelation 20:11), but Jesus' words remain. God is Lord of heaven and earth (see Matthew 11:25; Acts 17:24; Isaiah 66:1). His eternal sovereignty over both heaven and earth are affirmed and unquestioned.

Because God is in heaven, His revelation takes place from heaven (see Matthew 11:27). At Jesus' baptism, God's voice was heard from heaven (see Mark 1:11). The Holy Spirit came down from heaven (see Matthew 3:16). God's wrath goes forth from heaven, in the form of judgment against all evil, wickedness, unrighteousness, and ungodliness.

For the believers, the saints of God, there is the promise of salvation in heaven. Rewards and treasures are in heaven (see Matthew 6:20). The names of the disciples are recorded in heaven; their inheritance is in heaven; their citizenship or their home is in heaven (see Philippians 3:20). However, there is a heavenly Jerusalem which is also called the believer's true home (see Revelation 21:1-3) and even a temple in heaven (see Revelation 21:22). We can only conclude that the new heaven and the heavenly Jerusalem are the same. In the letter to the Church in Philadelphia, we find this promise (see Revelation 3:12).

We conclude this discussion of heaven. As we do, we remember that Jesus began His earthly ministry by proclaiming that the kingdom of heaven is near (see Matthew 4:17). So, it is clear that there is a direct relationship between Jesus, the Christ, and the kingdom of heaven. Let's examine that relationship.

THE REASONS JESUS CAME DOWN TO EARTH: HIS RELATIONSHIP TO THE CONCEPT OF HEAVEN

Consider Christ and His relationship to heaven. He came down from heaven. At His baptism, the heavens opened and the Holy Spirit descended on Him. Heaven opened above Him because He is the door of heaven and also the door of God's house on earth. Jesus Christ was acknowledged as the One whom God identified as His beloved Son. The eschatological events began in Him; in Christ, God was near.

"He [Jesus Christ] then added, 'I tell you the truth, you shall see heaven open, and the angels of God ascending and descending on the Son of Man'" (John 1:51). Notice: *on* the Son of Man.

We return to the concept of ascending and descending, for Christ is the spiritual ladder by which the redeemed and reconciled will ascend into heaven. Christ is not only the agent of creation (see 1 Corinthians 8:5-6; Colossians 1:15), but also, Christianity is founded on the basis that the belief in creation by God is consistent with the belief in Christ.

Consider Colossians 1:16, in which we see that Paul confirms all things were created by Him and for Him. I repeat, there is no belief in creation apart from belief in Jesus Christ. In addition, there is no belief in heaven apart from belief in Jesus Christ. It is the exalted Christ who has broken through the barriers erected by sinful mankind and the evil powers that isolated and separated man from God (see Ephesians 1:4-8; Romans 9:5). God has not established any barriers to His relationship with mankind: all barriers to redemption and reconciliation are those erected by mankind. Jesus came from heaven to remove all barriers and to justify (forgive, declare us innocent, and pardon) mankind, to redeem mankind, and to reconcile mankind to his Creator.

Three significant passages confirm these truths:

> For he [God] chose us in him [Christ] before the creation of the world to be holy and blameless in his sight. In love he predestined us to be adopted as his sons through Jesus Christ, in accordance with his pleasure and will—to the praise of his glorious grace, which he has freely given us in the One he loves. In him [Christ] we have redemption through his blood, the forgiveness of sins, in accordance with the riches of God's grace that he lavished on us with all wisdom and understanding.
>
> (Eph. 1:4-8)

> And when Jesus had cried out again in a loud voice, he gave up his spirit. At that moment the curtain of the temple was torn in two from top to bottom. The earth shook and the rocks split.
>
> (Matt. 27:50-52)

> Therefore, brothers, since we have confidence to enter the Most Holy Place by the blood of Jesus, by a new and living way opened for us through the curtain, that is, his body.
>
> (Heb. 10:19-20)

Jesus, the Son of God, came down from heaven to redeem and reconcile. He didn't redeem without the completing act of reconciling. As such, this is one of the most compelling ministries that Christ appointed for His church: that we would be His ministers of reconciliation (see 2 Corinthians 5:18). This ministry of reconciliation is that we would proclaim the Gospel message with confidence and boldness, that we would be faithful messengers of that truth, and that we would do all we could to encourage their commitment to Jesus Christ as Savior and Lord.

In summary, there is no belief in heaven apart from belief in Jesus Christ. Such is the heaven for which we pray. *Thy kingdom come on earth as it is in heaven.*

Our prayer is that heaven will come and its fullness will be evident now in the world in which we live. We look forward, with great expectation, to the Christ. *"He [Christ] who was seated on the throne said, 'I am making everything new!' Then he said, 'Write this down, for these words are trustworthy and true'"* (Revelation 21:5).

We will revisit this subject of heaven when we discuss the phrase, *"Thy will be done on earth as it is in heaven."*

As we continue our journey to explore the Person of God, Jesus now takes us to the next affirmation: *Hallowed be Thy name.*

Discussion Questions

1. What does it mean for God to be "in heaven"?

_____

_____

_____

_____

2. What is heaven?

_____

_____

_____

3. Where is heaven?

_____

_____

_____

4. How do you understand up and down as well as ascent and descent?

_____

_____

_____

_____

5. What is the progressive revelation of God?

_____

_____

_____

_____

6. What is the result of God being in heaven?

_____

_____

_____

_____

7. What is the relationship of Jesus Christ to heaven?

_____

_____

_____

_____

8. What does Colossians 1:15-20 tell you about the relationship of Jesus Christ to heaven?

_____

_____

_____

_____

9. Why did Jesus Christ come down from heaven?

_____

_____

_____

_____

10. What is the significance to you that you worship your Father, who is in heaven?

_____

_____

_____

_____

CHAPTER 5

HALLOWED BE THY NAME

HIS PERSON-3

After this manner therefore pray ye: Our Father who art in heaven, **Hallowed be thy name.** *Thy kingdom come. Thy will be done in earth, as it is in heaven. Give us this day our daily bread. And forgive us our debts, as we forgive our debtors. And lead us not into temptation, but deliver us from evil: For thine is the kingdom, and the power, and the glory, forever. Amen.*

O Lord, our Lord, how excellent is thy name in all the earth! who hast set thy glory above the heavens.

(Ps. 8:1 KJV)

JESUS SAID THAT the next thing we must do after we pray to our Father, who art in heaven, is to *hallow His name*. That immediately raises a series of questions. The first question is: what does it mean to hallow his name? If we are commanded to hallow His name, then that leads to the second question: Do we do that? I have to ask myself, Do I really hallow the name of God? Do I understand what I am saying? Do I really take this phrase seriously? Do I treat the name of God as a holy name and a holy thing? Or do I just slide on by this phrase without paying much attention to what I am saying?

So we come face to face with trying to understand and appreciate the significance of this term *hallow* and what it means to say to our Father, *hallowed be thy name?*

FIRST, WHAT DOES IT MEAN TO HALLOW HIS NAME?

This question is more important than the first question which is, How and why are we to hallow His name? To begin with, *hallow* is an anglicized form of the Hebrew word, *ha-lal'* or *hal'-el*, which means to set apart, consecrate, dedicate, sanctify, to consider sacred, to reverence as holy and to be separated from sinners in majesty, power, and sacredness. Above all, the word really means *"to praise."* From this Hebrew word, we get the anglicized word, *Hallelujah,* which is best translated *praise ye Yah, or Praise ye Yahweh.*

So above all else, *hallow* represents the revealed nature of God. What is that revealed nature? God has both a transferable nature and a non-transferable nature. When we grow into the image of God, we take on His transferable nature, which is His love, righteousness, patience, joy, and peace. These are characteristics that we are meant to seek and demonstrate in our lives. His non-transferable nature is His omnipotence, omniscience, and omnipresence. These are unique characteristics, and they are reserved for God alone. We are to hallow both His transferable and non-transferable natures. In addition, God has several names that reflect both His character and His nature.

We are not to profane, but we are to hallow His name.

Hear what the Word of God says, *"And you shall not profane my holy name; but I will be hallowed among the people of Israel"* (Leviticus 22:32 RSV). Again, we may ask, is that how I view God and the name of God? Looking more closely at the word, *ha-lal,* we find that the Psalms contain several groups of what are called the *Hallel,* or Hallelujah Psalms (see Psalms 107-150). Hallowing His name has always been important to the people of God. If we are to hallow His name today, there is no better source than these Psalms.

So that gives us a brief perspective of hallowed: Hallowed be thy name. Now let us look at the names of God, for it is His name that we are to hallow.

The Names of God that We Are to Hallow

The names of God define the character and the attributes of God. When we praise His name, we are offering praises for the significance of what His name implies or what He accomplishes in His name.

There are at least sixteen names used in Scripture for God, each conveying a unique aspect of His character. Some of the more common are the following five:

1. *Elohim*, "God": This is the most frequently used name in the Old Testament, as its equivalent *"theos"* (Greek), is in the New Testament. It is interesting to note that it is plural, pointing to and confirming the Trinitarian nature of the Godhead.
2. *Eloah*: The singular form of the name is confined in its use almost exclusively to poetic expression, being characteristic of the Book of Job.
3. *El*: In the group of Semitic languages, it is the most common word for deity (*el*). It is found throughout the Old Testament, but more often in Job and the Psalms than in all the other books.
4. *Adhon, Adhonay*: It is the generic name of God.
5. *Yahweh*: The name most distinctive of God as the God of Israel is Yahweh, a combination (YHWH) with the vowels of *Adhonay*, transliterated as *Yehowah*.

Although these five names represent the more common names for God, there are at least sixteen names for God given in the Old Testament:

Elohim: a reference to God's power and might
Adonai: Lord, a reference to the Lordship of God
Jehovah (Yahweh): a reference to God's divine salvation
Jehovah-Maccaddeshem: the Lord thy sanctifier
Jehovah-Rhodi: the Lord my shepherd
Jehovah-Sammah: the Lord who is present

Jehovah-Rapha: the Lord our healer
Jehovah-Tsidhena: the Lord our righteousness
Jehovah-Jireh:the Lord will provide
Jehovah-Nissi: the Lord our banner
Jehovah-Shalom: the Lord is peace
Jehovah-Sabbaoth: the Lord of hosts
El-Elyon: the most High God
El-Roi: the strong one who sees
El-Shaddai: God almighty
El-Olam: the everlasting God

The more foundational names are *El*, *Elohim* and, Jehovah (more correctly *Yahweh*). *Elohim* emphasizes the fullness of divine power while *Yahweh* identifies His divine preexistence and self-existence. These terms are varied or combined with others to bring out or emphasize certain attributes of the Godhead: e.g. God Almighty, the Living God, the Most High, the Lord, or the God of Hosts.

However, God has also given Himself a *"name."* In Exodus 3:13-15 it says, *"Moses said to God, 'Suppose I go to the Israelites and say to them, "The God of your fathers has sent me to you," and they ask me, "What is his name?" Then what shall I tell them?' God said to Moses, "I AM WHO I AM. This is what you are to say to the Israelites: 'I AM has sent me to you.'" God also said to Moses, "Say to the Israelites, 'The LORD, the God of your fathers—the God of Abraham, the God of Isaac and the God of Jacob—has sent me to you.'"* **This is my name forever, the name by which I am to be remembered from generation to generation.'"**

Is this name, *I AM WHO I AM*, uniquely different from all the other names of God that are identified in Scripture? I think not. This is the name He has given Himself. In addition, all the other names listed were used in special circumstances and for specific reasons.

This name, *I AM WHO I AM*, is a declaration that God said: I will be what I will be forever. That is a monumental truth, which can easily escape our understanding. Saying that, God has declared that He is the great *I AM*, and God said that is how He is to be remembered, forever. When Jesus came to earth, this is the same name, I AM, that Jesus Christ, God Incarnate, took and declared in His earthly ministry.

Jesus expresses His nature in the seven great I AM statements in the Gospel According to John:

1. *"Then Jesus declared, 'I am the bread of life.'"* (John 6:35-36, 51)
2. *"When Jesus spoke again to the people, he said, 'I am the light of the world.'"* (John 8:12)
3. *"Therefore Jesus said again, 'I tell you the truth, I am the gate for the sheep.'"* (John 10:7-11)
4. *"I am the good shepherd."* (John 10:14-16)
5. *"Jesus said to her, 'I am the resurrection and the life.'"* (John 11:25-26)
6. *"Jesus answered, 'I am the way and the truth and the life.'"* (John 14:6-7)
7. *"I am the vine; you are the branches."* (John 15:5-8)

The names of God have great meaning in the Bible as do all the men and women of the Bible. For example, notice how many names end in *el* (e.g. Daniel, Ezekiel), or *iah* for the first three letters of Yahweh (e.g. Isaiah, Jeremiah). Daniel means "God is my Judge." Ezekiel means "God strengthens." Isaiah means "the salvation of the Lord." Jeremiah means "the exaltation of the Lord." Every individual was, and is, given a name with eternal consequences. For example, Jesus was to be called *Emmanuel,* because He will save His people. In the book of Isaiah and in Revelation 3:12 we see that the Christ will be given a new name.

So we have examined the phrase, *hallowed be thy name.* We shall sing praises to Him and hold in awe and wonder the name of Him who is our Father. We have looked at three aspects of the Person of God: *Our Father which art in heaven, Hallowed be thy name.* We now turn to the next phrase, *"Thy kingdom come,"* as we continue to explore the Person of God.

Discussion Questions

1. What does it means to *"hallow"* the name of God?

_____

_____

_____

_____

2. What are the Hallel Psalms?

_____

_____

_____

3. Read Psalm 110, the coming of the Priest-King-Judge. What single message do you understand from this Psalm?

_____

_____

_____

4. Read Psalm 113. What single message do you gather from this Psalm?

_____

_____

_____

_____

5. Read Psalm 119. What does the "Word of the Lord" mean?

_____

_____

_____

_____

6. Read Psalm 121. This is a song of ascent. What do you learn about God in this Psalm?

_____

_____

_____

_____

7. Read Psalm 133. What is the message of this Psalm?

_____

_____

_____

_____

8. What are five important names of God that we are to hallow?

_____

_____

_____

9. What is the meaning/significance of each of these names?

_____

_____

_____

_____

10. What is the name that God has given Himself?

_____

_____

_____

11. How is that name preserved in the New Testament?

_____

_____

_____

12. How does Jesus Christ use that name in the proclamation of His identity? What are seven ways He used that name?

_____

_____

_____

_____

CHAPTER 6

THY KINGDOM COME
HIS PERSON-4

After this manner therefore pray ye: Our Father which art in heaven, Hallowed be thy name. **Thy kingdom come.** *Thy will be done in earth, as it is in heaven. Give us this day our daily bread. And forgive us our debts, as we forgive our debtors. And lead us not into temptation, but deliver us from evil: For thine is the kingdom, and the power, and the glory, forever. Amen.*

All you have made will praise you, O LORD; your saints will extol you. They will tell of the glory of your kingdom and speak of your might, so that all men may know of your mighty acts and the glorious splendor of your kingdom. Your kingdom is an everlasting kingdom, and your dominion endures through all generations.

(Ps. 145:10-13)

"The time has come," he [Jesus Christ] said. "The kingdom of God is near. Repent and believe the good news!"

(Mark 1:15)

Once, having been asked by the Pharisees when the kingdom of God would come, Jesus replied, "The kingdom of God does not come with your careful observation, nor will people say, 'Here it is,' or 'There it is,' because the kingdom of God is within you."

(Luke 17:20-21)

THESE FEW SCRIPTURAL passages present a brief, but interesting, overall perspective of the kingdom of God. First, the kingdom of God is an everlasting kingdom; second, the nearness of the kingdom of God is good news; third, the kingdom of God is within each of us; fourth, we must endure many hardships before we can enter the kingdom of God (see Acts 14:22); fifth, flesh and blood cannot enter the kingdom of God—only those born of the Spirit will inherit the kingdom of God (see 1 Corinthians 15:50).

In addition, there are two specific aspects of the kingdom of God that we must recognize. First, it is God's kingdom that we pray for; it is not our kingdom; second, we seek for God's kingdom to *come* and be evident on earth now and forever. The kingdom of God is mentioned twice in this prayer: at this juncture and as the closing phrase in the prayer.

With that in mind, we will examine nine questions in order to understand the importance that Christ places on this theme: What is the kingdom of God? What is the purpose of the kingdom of God? Where is the kingdom of God? Who are the citizens of the kingdom? What are the characteristics of the kingdom of God? What is Jesus' teaching on the kingdom of God? What are the parables of Jesus that specifically relate to the kingdom? What is the spiritual and historical perspective of the kingdom of God? Why do we pray for the kingdom of God to come to earth?

Let us address each of these nine questions in order.

What Is the Kingdom of God?

In the most direct form, the kingdom of God is that moral and spiritual kingdom which the God of grace is establishing in this fallen world, whose citizens are those who willingly accept His sovereign authority and power, and of which His Son Jesus is the glorified Head.

In the truest sense, this kingdom has existed ever since there were men who walked with God (see Genesis 5:24), who waited for His salvation (see Genesis 49:18), who knew that, "*I [God] am always with you; you hold me by my right hand*" (*Psalm 73:23*), and who knew that, even in the valley of the shadow of death feared no evil, when He was with them (see Psalm 23:4).

There has always been this perspective of the kingdom of God. However, the true and complete kingdom awaits the Second Coming of the Messiah, the Christ. When Messiah Himself appeared at His first coming, the kingdom was at hand. It was visible in Jesus Christ, who, as the King of the kingdom, was also at hand. His earthly life, crucifixion, and death laid the foundations for His resurrection and ascension to heaven where He is now seated in glory at the right hand of the Father. At His first coming, Jesus Christ came as Savior; at His second coming, He will come as King and Judge.

The presence of the kingdom of God in this world forever controls the course of human life and human history (see Matthew 13:24-33). The Son of God is the King of the kingdom. When the Son has accomplished His rule, He will return the kingdom to the Father (see 1 Corinthians 15:23-28).

With this understanding, the next question deals with the purpose of the kingdom.

WHAT IS THE PURPOSE OF THE KINGDOM?

The purpose of the kingdom is the *forgiveness, redemption, justification, propitiation, and reconciliation* of all mankind and deliverance from the powers of evil (see 1 Corinthians 15:23-28). Therefore, His kingdom is the redemptive rule of God in Christ, defeating Satan and the powers of evil and delivering mankind from corruption. It brings to mankind *"righteousness, peace and joy in the Holy Spirit" (Romans 14:17)*. By entering the kingdom, the righteous will be delivered from the powers of darkness, *"For he has rescued us from the dominion of darkness and brought us into the kingdom of the Son he loves, in whom we have redemption, the forgiveness of sins" (Colossians 1:13-14)*.

Forgiveness means that God accepts the death of His Son on the Cross as full and complete satisfaction to meet the demands of God's holiness and righteousness. The believer is assured, accompanied by

59

his confession and repentance, that he is forgiven of all his sins—past, present, and future—for there is no condemnation for those who are in Christ (see Romans 8:1; Colossians 2:13; John 3:18).

Redemption means that a ransom has been paid for our release from any authority or power other than that of God. Redemption requires the confession and repentance of our sins and involves the full payment by another for our sins. Redemption represents the special intervention by God for the salvation of mankind. That intervention is through the cross and the atoning sacrifice of Christ, by virtue of which Christ is called our Redeemer.

Justification means that the judgment of our Holy God declares a confessing and repentant sinner to be pardoned, declared innocent, righteous and acceptable before Him because Christ has borne the sinner's sin on the cross.

Propitiation involves the manner in which a holy God deals with unholy subjects. Propitiation stands for two ideas: First, it stands for the atoning death of Jesus on the cross, through which He paid the penalty demanded by God because of man's sin, thus setting mankind free from sin and death. Second, it also expresses the truth that Christ has turned aside the wrath of God against sin. Christ is our advocate, and He is the perfect sacrifice for the sins of the world.

Reconciliation means that God has taken the initiative in a world that has been alienated from God. He reestablished fellowship with His created. Jesus Christ is the one who reconciles us to God. As such, citizens of the kingdom are to be ambassadors of reconciliation (see 2 Corinthians 5:20).

These five words: *forgiveness, redemption, justification, propitiation, and reconciliation,* represent the purpose for the kingdom of God. If that is the purpose of the kingdom, then where is the kingdom?

WHERE IS THE KINGDOM OF GOD?

We must recognize several points as we address this question. First, God is spirit (see John 4:24); second, the kingdom of God is not of this world; third, the King of the kingdom is Jesus, the Christ; fourth, the kingdom is the eternal dominion of God, which is an everlasting kingdom. So where is the kingdom of God? It is with the King. Wherever the King is, there will be the kingdom. Jesus said that if the Spirit of God is within you, then the kingdom is within you.

> *Once, having been asked by the Pharisees when the kingdom of God would come, Jesus replied, "The kingdom of God does not come with your careful observation, nor will people say, 'Here it is,' or 'There it is,' because the kingdom of God is within you."*
>
> (Luke 17:20-21)

> *And if the Spirit of him who raised Jesus from the dead is living in you, he who raised Christ from the dead will also give life to your mortal bodies through his Spirit, who lives in you.*
>
> (Rom. 8:11)

> *Don't you know that you yourselves are God's temple and that God's Spirit lives in you?*
>
> (1 Cor. 3:16)

> *I write to you, young men, because you are strong, and the word of God lives in you, and you have overcome the evil one.*
>
> (1 John 2:14)

> *You, however, are controlled not by the sinful nature but by the Spirit, if the Spirit of God lives in you. And if anyone does not have the Spirit of Christ, he does not belong to Christ.*
>
> (Rom. 8:9)

> *No one has ever seen God; but if we love one another, God lives in us and his love is made complete in us.*
>
> (1 John 4:12)

Hear the multiple truths: God lives in us; the Spirit of God lives within us; the word of God lives within us; the kingdom of God is within us. You and I represent the kingdom of God, if the Spirit of God is in us. That is an amazing thought, an amazing challenge, and an amazing responsibility.

Even as we are citizens and heirs of the kingdom, we are to witness to the kingdom. We are the kingdom, living under the authority of our King, our God, our Savior and our Lord, and in the power of the Spirit. We show it by who we are and by what we do. I have to ask myself, "Is that how I live? Is that how I represent the kingdom?" So Jesus said that the answer to the question, *Where is the kingdom?* is, *It is within you.* So with this introduction, the next question is equally direct.

WHO ARE THE CITIZENS OF THE KINGDOM?

They are the ones who have been justified, who have been redeemed, who are the saints of the Lord, and who have been reconciled to the God and Father of us all. They are witnesses and ambassadors. They are the ones who do the Father's will. So if this is the kingdom and its purpose and the kingdom is within us, then what are the characteristics of the kingdom to which we are to bear witness?

WHAT ARE THE CHARACTERISTICS OF THE KINGDOM OF GOD?

Scripture identifies at least six significant characteristics of the kingdom of God. Let us consider each of these in order.

1. IT IS AN EVERLASTING KINGDOM.

   Then the sovereignty, power and greatness of the kingdoms under the whole heaven will be handed over to the saints, the people of the Most High. His kingdom will be an everlasting kingdom, and all rulers will worship and obey him.

   (Dan. 7:27)

2. IT IS A KINGDOM IN WHICH ALL THE NATIONS OF THE EARTH WILL BE UNDER THE LORDSHIP OF GOD.

   They will proclaim my glory among the nations. And they will bring all your brothers, from all the nations, to my holy mountain in Jerusalem as an offering to the LORD.

   (Isa. 66:19-20)

3. IT IS A KINGDOM WHICH WE MUST SEEK.

But seek first his kingdom and his righteousness, and all these things will be given to you as well.

(Matt. 6:33)

4. IT IS A KINGDOM THAT WE MUST ENTER WITH CHILDLIKE SIMPLICITY.

He [Jesus] said to them, "Let the little children come to me, and do not hinder them, for the kingdom of God belongs to such as these. I tell you the truth, anyone who will not receive the kingdom of God like a little child will never enter it.

(Mark 10:14-15)

5. IT IS A KINGDOM NOT OF THIS WORLD.

When Jesus said that His kingdom was not of this world, He meant that it was not derived from earthly authorities but from God; it is not like a human or earthly kingdom. Jesus said, "My kingdom is not of this world. If it were, my servants would fight to prevent my arrest by the Jews. But now my kingdom is from another place."

(John 18:36)

6. IT IS A KINGDOM IN WHICH WE MUST BE *BORN AGAIN* TO SEE AND ENTER.

In reply Jesus declared, "I tell you the truth, no one can see the kingdom of God unless he is born again." "How can a man be born when he is old?" Nicodemus asked. "Surely he cannot enter a second time into his mother's womb to be born!" Jesus answered, "I tell you the truth, no one can enter the kingdom of God unless he is born of water and the Spirit."

(John 3:3-6)

WHAT ARE THE TEACHINGS OF JESUS REGARDING THE KINGDOM?

It is interesting to see that Jesus taught in two distinct ways regarding the kingdom of God. First, His message was direct and explicit. Second, after His rejection by the Jews, Jesus taught in parables.

The kingdom of God becomes the comprehensive term for the entirety of Jesus' teaching. At the beginning of His ministry, *"Jesus went throughout Galilee, teaching in their synagogues, preaching the good news [the gospel] of the kingdom, and healing every disease and sickness among the people"* (Matthew 4:23).

In Luke 8:1, Luke tells us, *"After this, Jesus traveled about from one town and village to another, proclaiming the good news of the kingdom of God. The Twelve were with him."*

During Jesus' earthly ministry, His primary teaching regarding the kingdom of God is best contained in one passage. *"But seek first his kingdom and his righteousness, and all these things will be given to you as well"* (Matthew 6:33). All these things are all the economic, social, and physical needs that we face daily in this world. Jesus said, *"All these things will be given to you as well."*

With the coming of Jesus, the Christ, He brought an expanded and universal view of the kingdom, in contrast to the nationalistic view of the Jews.

The Jews were thinking of a natural and physical kingdom with a human king, governed by human laws and with limited and specific national boundaries. Their thinking was restrictive and related directly to the kingdom of the Israelites. As a result, when the Jews spoke of the kingdom of God, they were thinking primarily of a national Jewish kingdom that would free the Jews from Roman domination, reestablish the glory of David, and establish a kingdom with a Jewish king and court—a kingdom that would lead to a worldwide dominion going forth from Mt. Zion.

This misconception existed even among Christ's followers, as illustrated by their question after His resurrection and just before His ascension. Luke reports this in Acts 1:6-8, *"So when they met together, they asked him, 'Lord, are you at this time going to restore the kingdom to Israel?' He said to them: 'It is not for you to know the times or dates the Father has set by his own authority. But you will receive power when the Holy Spirit comes on you; and you will be my witnesses in Jerusalem, and in all Judea and Samaria, and to the ends of the earth.'"*

His disciples asked if Jesus was going to restore the kingdom to Israel now. Jesus said that he was not talking about the physical kingdom of Israel; he was talking about the spiritual kingdom of God. Jesus was speaking of a spiritual kingdom, without physical boundaries, whose King is Jesus Christ, whose governance would be according to the laws of God, and whose citizens would be those who had received Jesus Christ as Savior and Lord. Jesus was proclaiming that God was actively directing the course of history for all nations. This inclusion of all nations is what Paul called *the great mystery, hidden for ages.*

> *Now to him who is able to establish you by my gospel and the proclamation of Jesus Christ, according to the revelation of the mystery hidden for long ages past, but now revealed and made known through the prophetic writings by the command of the eternal God, so that all nations might believe and obey him—to the only wise God be glory forever through Jesus Christ! Amen.*
> (Rom. 16:25-27)

The mystery is that all nations might believe and obey Him [God]. God had never been only the God of the Jews; God has been and will always be the God of all nations. However, from all the nations of the world, the Jews were God's chosen people, and they were chosen for a purpose. Their purpose was to be a witness to the glory, majesty, and power of God. However, God is the Creator of all; He is the source of all life. All nations are under His authority, power, and control, whether they know it or not.

In like manner, Abraham was to be the father of many nations, not just of the Israelites. God could make that covenant promise because God is forever the God of all the nations. However, God was faithful in keeping the covenant with Abraham, even though the Israelites had been unfaithful in their relationship with God.

Moreover, the preeminent commandment for including all nations in the kingdom of God is that given by Jesus in Matthew 28:18-20, "*Then Jesus came to them and said, 'All authority in heaven and on earth has been given to me. Therefore go and make disciples of all nations, baptizing them in the name of the Father and of the Son and of the Holy Spirit, and teaching them to obey everything I have commanded you. And surely I am with you always, to the very end of the age.'"*

The teachings of Jesus were that the kingdom of God had come in the Person of the Son of God, that the kingdom would include and represent all nations, that the church is to make disciples of all nations, that the kingdom would be an everlasting kingdom, that the kingdom would not be of this world, that it would be spiritual in nature, and that the marks of the kingdom would be righteousness, love, unity, joy, and peace.

Jesus not only taught directly about the kingdom, but He also used parables to explain the character of the kingdom that He had come to proclaim.

WHAT PARABLES OF JESUS SPECIFICALLY RELATE TO THE KINGDOM OF GOD?

Jesus presented the ideal and character of the kingdom of God in a series of parables. I have previously published a book, *God's Hidden Treasure: The Parables of Jesus*, in which I discussed all of His thirty-four parables, including the seventeen that dealt, directly or indirectly, with the kingdom of God. I am quoting now from my book:

> However, before looking at the parables, we should understand this kingdom to which Jesus directs our attention. To begin with, the kingdom is called by various terms, e.g. the kingdom of Heaven, thy kingdom, His kingdom, the kingdom of my Father, the kingdom of God, and the kingdom of Jesus Christ. These all mean the same thing, but it is important to note that Jesus constantly refers to it as the kingdom of God (3 times in Matthew, 14 times in Mark, 32 times in Luke, and 2 times in John). By contrast, the kingdom of Heaven in mentioned 32 times in Matthew and not at all in the other three versions of the Gospel. The gospel is the gospel of the kingdom, the word of the kingdom; in the same manner, the inhabitants of the kingdom are called the sons of the kingdom. The kingdom of heaven is that universal kingdom that is present wherever the sovereign God reigns and His righteousness, love, joy, and peace are evident.

It is universal in the plan of God that all nations should flow to His holy hill and be His children in His kingdom. The kingdom denotes God's sovereignty and loving power that can never pass away. The kingdom of God has its King, the sovereign God, who has eternally been the King of His people.

In the parables, Jesus proclaimed that the kingdom of God is present in His own Person and through His Word (see Matthew 13:3-9, 18-23). The kingdom is present because Jesus Christ, the King, is present. The King is where His kingdom is; the kingdom is where the King is. Its growth is inevitable because God is sovereign and His will for His kingdom is certain to be fulfilled. The kingdom is present now, but not in its fullness, for the final manifestation of the kingdom will occur when Christ shall return in all His glory (see Matthew 25:31-36).

We all must recognize that Jesus introduces this thought of the kingdom of God in the opening phrases of the prayer. We also want to be aware that this theme, the kingdom of God, will appear again in the conclusion of the prayer. So the question before us is: Why do we pray for the kingdom of God to come to earth?

Why Do We Pray for the Kingdom of God to Come to Earth?

A series of questions come to mind: Are you satisfied with the way you are living your life under secular authority? Do you like the people who are governing you? Is something missing? Do you want laws to be more just and more righteous? Do you want a way of life that is richer and more rewarding and offers some tangible eternal benefits? Do you want different standards of conduct by which you live in your society? What is missing? What is wrong with the present level of civilization? These are important questions; they deserve thoughtful consideration.

The history of civilization does not present a pretty picture. Take every empire and kingdom from the beginning of time. Consider the Assyrians, Babylonians, Egyptians, Romans, and coming to more contemporary times—the British Empire, and to the Third Reich.

The list is endless with few examples of lasting greatness, in which peace among nations or individual human dignity is ever realized. Instead, the story is filled with the examples of great empires that have never come close to meeting true human interests and needs. The history of empires is a story of abusive power, greed, corruption, exploitation, and cruelty that defies description. Earthly kingdoms, at best, have proven to be bankrupt societies with little regard for any reasonable interest in the life of their citizens.

Is that too harsh a condemnation? I think not.

Is it possible that the kingdom Scripture describes is a far better kingdom than man can devise? Is it possible that God's laws and commandments are more beneficial to everyone? Is it possible that God's justice might be more equitable? Is it possible that unity and love might dominate the kingdom? Is it possible that true peace might prevail? Is it possible that man might love his fellow man and that the lion might lie down with the lamb? The answers to these questions are abundantly clear—at least to me. I want the kingdom of God, as explained so well in Scripture, to come.

In summary, we conclude the following:

- The everlasting, eternal, spiritual kingdom has always been on the heart of God.
- His plan is for all the people of all the nations.
- The kingdom is within those who are disciples of Jesus Christ.
- The purpose of the kingdom is redemption, justification, propitiation, and reconciliation, leading to eternal life.
- God is the King of all the nations.

I pray for the kingdom to come, because I believe that God's kingdom is the only one in which I want to live. It is the only one that truly offers and can guarantee love and respect among nations. Therefore, I pray: *Thy kingdom come.*

Discussion Questions

1. What is the kingdom of God?

_____

_____

_____

_____

2. What is the purpose of the kingdom?

_____

_____

_____

_____

3. Where is the kingdom of God (Luke 17:20-21)?

_____

_____

_____

_____

4. Who are the citizens of the kingdom?

_____

_____

_____

_____

5. How do you become a citizen of the kingdom?

_____

_____

_____

_____

6. What are at least six characteristics of the kingdom?

_____

_____

_____

_____

7. What are the teachings of Jesus Christ regarding the kingdom?

_____

_____

_____

_____

8. What is the great mystery, hidden for ages?

_____

_____

_____

_____

9. What parables directly relate to the kingdom of God?

_____

_____

_____

_____

10. Why do you pray for the coming of the kingdom?

_____

_____

_____

_____

CHAPTER 7

THY WILL BE DONE IN EARTH, AS IT IS IN HEAVEN

THE PERSON—5

*After this manner therefore pray ye: Our Father which art in heaven, Hallowed be thy name. Thy kingdom come. **Thy will be done in earth, as it is in heaven.** Give us this day our daily bread. And forgive us our debts, as we forgive our debtors. And lead us not into temptation, but deliver us from evil: For thine is the kingdom, and the power, and the glory, forever. Amen.*

*For I [Jesus Christ] have come down from heaven not to do my will but to do the will of him who sent me. And this is the will of him who sent me, that I shall lose none of all that he has given me, but raise them up at the last day. For my **Father's will is that everyone who looks to the Son and believes in him shall have eternal life,** and I will raise him up at the last day.*

(John 6:38-40)

The world and its desires pass away, but the man who does the will of God lives forever.

(1 John 2:17)

May the God of peace, who through the blood of the eternal covenant brought back from the dead our Lord Jesus, that great Shepherd of the sheep, equip you with everything good for doing his will, and may he work in us what is pleasing to him, through Jesus Christ, to whom be glory for ever and ever. Amen.

(Heb. 13:20-21)

CONSIDER THE IMPORTANT messages in the passages above. Jesus said, *"For I have come down from heaven not to do my will but to do the will of him who sent me"* (John 6:38). Also, it is the Father's will that everyone who believes in the Son will have eternal life (see John 6:40). It is the Father's will that the person who does the will of God would live forever (see 1 John 2:17). Jesus said that his *food* was to do the will of the One who had sent him (see John 4:34). It is the will of God to equip the saints for every good work (see Hebrews 13:21). These are only a few passages that touch upon this vital topic.

Now, this subject, the will of God in heaven and on earth, can be approached only with the greatest of humility. It is a serious matter to presume to understand fully the will of God. When you first look at this petition, *thy will be done on earth as it is in heaven,* this phrase may seem like a piece of cake; it's no big deal. However, I have to tell you that this phrase is one of the more difficult passages in Scripture.

Today, Jesus directs us to pray for His will in heaven to be also done here on earth. Because Jesus asks us to pray in this manner, then He knows this is possible. If Jesus knows it is possible, then I also have to believe it will be done.

To understand this phrase, *Thy will be done on earth as it is in heaven,* we need to examine three major subjects: First, the doctrine of reconciliation; second, the doctrine of the will of God; third, examples of the will of God. I am convinced that the Word of God leads us to at least four basic truths, of which the last two truths are closely interrelated.

First, we cannot understand the will of God until we have accepted Jesus Christ as Savior and Lord and have been reconciled to our Father. We can't be reconciled unless we are in His will. His will is not known unless we are reconciled.

Second, God primarily reveals His will only to His children, those who are *born again.*

74

Third, reconciliation and the will of God are two closely interconnected doctrines; we must understand one to understand the other.

Fourth, obeying His will leads to more complete reconciliation; being reconciled to God opens the window to understanding more fully His will.

The key in the prayer is this: reconciliation foreshadows our understanding of His will. In the same way, knowing and following the will of God increases the depth of our relationship and fellowship with God and the degree of our reconciliation.

Paul and the author of Hebrews recognize that maturity in Christ is an ongoing process. The more mature we become, the more we are reconciled to God and to each other. The more reconciled we become, the more we become equipped to understand the will of God in a greater way. Knowing God's will and reconciliation are ongoing and progressive stages of Christian growth. Let me share three passages regarding the progressive change in people as they grow into maturity.

Him we proclaim, warning every man and teaching every man in all wisdom, that we may present every man mature in Christ.

(Col. 1:28 RSV)

Brothers, I could not address you as spiritual but as worldly— mere infants in Christ. I gave you milk, not solid food, for you were not yet ready for it. Indeed, you are still not ready. You are still worldly.

(1 Cor. 3:1-3)

In fact, though by this time you ought to be teachers, you need someone to teach you the elementary truths of God's word all over again. You need milk, not solid food! Anyone who lives on milk, being still an infant, is not acquainted with the teaching about righteousness. But solid food is for the mature, who by constant use have trained themselves to distinguish good from evil.

(Heb. 5:12-14)

Maturity in Christ is necessary to achieve a fuller reconciliation with God; in turn, reconciliation is a necessary prelude to knowing God's will. Therefore, let us examine the Doctrine of Reconciliation before examining the Doctrine of the Will of God.

THE DOCTRINE OF RECONCILIATION

The understanding of the doctrine of reconciliation will provide the basis of our understanding of the will of God in heaven that we pray will come on earth. If we truly want His will to be done on earth as it is in heaven, then we must demonstrate that we seek nothing more, nothing less, than full and complete reconciliation with God, our Father. The key then for fulfilling His will on earth is *reconciliation*.

To begin with, God wants us to be reconciled to Him and to each other. Two passages highlight this truth:

Not only is this so, but we also rejoice in God through our Lord Jesus Christ, through whom we have now received reconciliation.
(Rom. 5:11)

All this is from God, who reconciled us to himself through Christ and gave us the ministry of reconciliation: that God was reconciling the world to himself in Christ, not counting men's sins against them. And he has committed to us the message of reconciliation. We are therefore Christ's ambassadors, as though God were making his appeal through us. We implore you on Christ's behalf: Be reconciled to God.
(2 Cor. 5:18-20)

These two passages make reconciliation abundantly clear. First, it is through Jesus Christ that we have received reconciliation (Romans 5:11); second, Paul restates this important truth: that God is reconciling the world to Himself in Christ (2 Corinthians 5:18-20).

Paul cites six steps in the reconciliation process. First, God has taken the initiative to reconcile us to Himself; second, it is through Christ that we receive reconciliation; third, God does not count our sins against us; fourth, God has given us the message of reconciliation; fifth, we are Christ's ambassadors with the message of reconciliation, and, sixth, God is making His appeal to others through us.

So what is the reconciliation that God has initiated? Theological dictionaries define reconciliation simply as the process by which a holy God and sinful man are reunited. Man is a sinner. He is disobedient and rebellious; it is his nature. All have sinned and fallen short of the glory of God (see Romans 3:23).

The Bible teaches that God and man are alienated from one another because of God's holiness and man's sinfulness. This contrast, between holiness and sinfulness, forces God to face the divine dilemma. How does the holy God deal justly with sinful man? Although God loves the sinner (see Romans 5:8), it is impossible for Him to ignore sin (see Hebrews 10:27). Therefore, in biblical reconciliation, both parties are affected. Through the sacrifice of Christ, man's sin is atoned, and God's wrath against sin is turned aside. This is propitiation. Thereby, a relationship of hostility and alienation is transformed into a relationship of love, unity, peace, and fellowship.

The initiative in reconciliation has been taken by God while we were yet sinners. We were worse than sinners; we were enemies of God (see Romans 5:10). In spite of that, Christ died for us (see Romans 5:8, Colossians 1:21-22). Reconciliation is God's own completed act; God Himself has reconciled us to Himself through Jesus Christ (see 2 Corinthians 5:18).

God paid a tremendous price to achieve reconciliation. The price was the death of Christ on the cross for your sins and my sins. The cross demonstrates at least two things: first, it reveals the depth of God's love and His desire for reconciliation; second, it reveals the magnitude of our sins.

If we pray in this prayer—*that His will be done on earth as it is in heaven*—then we can only do so on the basis of reconciliation with God and our fellow man. It follows then that only when we have been reconciled to God and to one another can we begin to understand the nature of God's will.

We move to that subject now.

THE DOCTRINE OF THE WILL OF GOD

In The Lord's Prayer, we are praying for His will—not your will or my will. We are praying for His will to be done—accomplished where and in whom and by whatever means He chooses.

The word, *done* means *made complete in me.* But how are we to understand the word *will*? In Scripture, the word is understood as both a verb and a noun. As a verb, the word chiefly rendered here is *to long for.* God *longs for* a relationship with His created. Why else would He send His Son to die on the cross, if not to reconcile mankind to Himself? So the first question is: What is God's will in heaven that we seek here on earth?

I think the Bible shows us that in heaven, God's will is reflected in righteousness, love unbounded, joy in fellowship, and a relationship unparalleled in holiness. In heaven, God is honored, worshipped, and praised constantly. Is that what we have on earth? Is that what we want on earth?

In many regards, God's will in heaven has already been revealed through the coming of His Son. For that reason, His will in heaven is that His creation would be reconciled to Him.

I emphasize again, it is only through the power of the Holy Spirit that we can be reconciled and know the will of God. The Spirit, who indwells us, is the One who leads us into all truth.

The will of God is multifaceted, and is best understood by the expression of His will in many areas: e.g. the overall will of God, for His Son, for His saints, for unbelievers, for His church, for His Spirit, and for His creation. We shall look at each area briefly.

THE OVERALL WILL OF GOD

His Will is for the complete harmony of heaven and earth in which His love, truth, holiness, righteousness, goodness, and justice are evident. Examples of the will of God are as follows:

- His preeminent will is to redeem His creation, primarily through the salvation of all people and for them to come to knowledge of the truth. *"I [Paul] urge, then, first of all, that requests, prayers, intercession and thanksgiving be made for everyone—for kings and all those in authority, that we may live peaceful and quiet lives in all godliness and holiness. This is good, and pleases God our Savior, who wants all men to be saved and to come to a knowledge of the truth"* (1 Timothy 2:1-4).

- His will for His chosen people is that all they do would be for His glory. *"In him we were also chosen, having been predestined according to the plan of him who works out everything in conformity with the purpose of his will, in order that we, who were the first to hope in Christ, might be for the praise of his glory"* (Ephesians 1:11-13).
- God's will is that all the nations would worship Him. *"All the nations you have made will come and worship before you, O Lord; they will bring glory to your name. For you are great and do marvelous deeds; you alone are God"* (Psalm 86:9-10).
- His will is to give eternal life. *"My Father's will is that everyone who looks to the Son and believes in him shall have eternal life, and I [Christ] will raise him up at the last day"* (John 6:38-40).
- It was the Father's will that the Son should die for the sins of the World. *"And we have seen and testify that the Father has sent his Son to be the Savior of the world. If anyone acknowledges that Jesus is the Son of God, God lives in him and he in God"* (1 John 4:14-16).

Other examples of His will are that none should perish (see 2 Peter 3:9); for us to do good works (see Ephesians 2:8-10); to reveal Himself to those who did not seek Him (see Isaiah 65:1); to be found by all who seek Him (see Jeremiah 29:13-14); that all people would be reconciled to Him though His Son (see 2 Corinthians 5:18-20); that we would hear the word of God and obey it (see Luke 11:28); and that our worship of Him would be in spirit and in truth. (see John 4:23-24)

Next, let us examine God's will for His Son.

THE WILL OF GOD FOR HIS SON

His will for His Son is to do the will of the Father. *"Yet not my will, but yours [God, the Father] be done." (Luke 22:42)*

God's will is that His Son would be glorified by all people in every nation. *"That at the name of Jesus every knee should bow, in heaven and on earth and under the earth, and every tongue confess that Jesus Christ is Lord, to the glory of God the Father"* (Philippians 2:10-11).

God's will is that the Son would die for the sins of the world. *"He is the atoning sacrifice for our sins, and not only for ours but also for the sins of the whole world"* (1 John 2:2).

God's will is that Christ would seek and save the lost. *"For the Son of Man came to seek and to save what was lost"* (Luke 19:10).

His will for His Christ is to destroy the works of the devil. *"The reason the Son of God appeared was to destroy the devil's work"* (1 John 3:8).

His will is that Christ would testify to the truth. *"Jesus answered, 'You [Pilate] are right in saying I am a king. In fact, for this reason I was born, and for this I came into the world, to testify to the truth. Everyone on the side of truth listens to me'"* (John 18:37).

God's will is that His Son would be honored as the Head of the church (see Colossians 1:18); that we would be reconciled to God through His Son (see 2 Corinthians 5:18-20); that Christ would cleanse our conscience, so that we may serve God (see Hebrews 9:14); and that all things will be united in His Son (see Ephesians 1:9-13).

Next, let us consider God's will for His Spirit.

THE WILL OF GOD FOR HIS SPIRIT

The Spirit intercedes for the saints.

"In the same way, the Spirit helps us in our weakness. We do not know what we ought to pray for, but the Spirit himself intercedes for us with groans that words cannot express. And he who searches our hearts knows the mind of the Spirit, because the Spirit intercedes for the saints in accordance with God's will."

(Rom. 8:26-27)

The Holy Spirit will lead us into all truth. He will bring glory to Christ.

> *"But when he, the Spirit of truth, comes, he will guide you into all truth. He will not speak on his own; he will speak only what he hears, and he will tell you what is yet to come. He will bring glory to me by taking from what is mine and making it known to you. All that belongs to the Father is mine. That is why I said the Spirit will take from what is mine and make it known to you."*
>
> (John 16:13-15)

THE WILL OF GOD FOR HIS SAINTS, THE REDEEMED OF THE LORD

God's will for the saints is that we would grow into the image of God. *"Then God said, 'Let us make man in our image, in our likeness'"* (Genesis 1:26).

God's will is that we should commit the rest of our lives to do the will of God. *"He does not live the rest of his earthly life for evil human desires, but rather for the will of God"* (1 Peter 4:2).

God's will is that we would know that He created us to do good works, which He has prepared for us. *"For we are God's workmanship, created in Christ Jesus to do good works, which God prepared in advance for us to do"* (Ephesians 2:10).

God's will for His people is to be joyful, pray without ceasing, and give thanks in all circumstances. *"Be joyful always; pray continually; give thanks in all circumstances, for this is God's will for you in Christ Jesus"* (1 Thessalonians 5:16-18).

God's will is that we would become mature in Christ. *"Him we proclaim, warning every man and teaching every man in all wisdom, that we may present every man mature in Christ"* (Colossians 1:28 RSV).

God's will is that our priority is to seek first His kingdom. *"Seek first his kingdom and his righteousness"* (Matthew 6:33).

God's will is that we would have an inclusive love, a love that includes our enemies. *"But I tell you: Love your enemies and pray for those who persecute you, that you may be sons of your Father in heaven"* (Matthew 5:44-45).

81

God's will is that we obey the two great commandments. "'*Love the Lord your God with all your heart and with all your soul and with all your mind.' This is the first and greatest commandment. And the second is like it: 'Love your neighbor as yourself.' All the Law and the Prophets hang on these two commandments*" (Matthew 22:37-40).

God's will is that we submit ourselves to God, resist the devil, and come near to God. "*Submit yourselves, then, to God. Resist the devil, and he will flee from you. Come near to God and he will come near to you*" (James 4:7-8).

God's will is that we honor the ministry of reconciliation that has been entrusted to us. "*All this is from God, who reconciled us to himself through Christ and gave us the ministry of reconciliation: that God was reconciling the world to himself in Christ, not counting men's sins against them. And he has committed to us the message of reconciliation. We are therefore Christ's ambassadors, as though God were making his appeal through us. We implore you on Christ's behalf: Be reconciled to God*" (2 Corinthians 5:18-20).

God's will is that we be transformed. "*Do not conform any longer to the pattern of this world, but be transformed by the renewing of your mind. Then you will be able to test and approve what God's will is—his good, pleasing and perfect will*" (Romans 12:2).

God's will is that we would be His witnesses to the ends of the earth. "*But you will receive power when the Holy Spirit comes on you; and you will be my witnesses in Jerusalem, and in all Judea and Samaria, and to the ends of the earth*" (Acts 1:8).

His will is that we not serve other gods (see Joshua 24:15); that we serve God, not men (see Ephesians 6:7-8); that Christ would cleanse our conscience, so that we may better serve God (see Hebrews 9:14); that we would focus on serving the Lord (see Colossians 3:23-25); that we would know that we have been equipped to do His will (see Hebrews 13:20-21); that we would humble ourselves, pray, seek the face of God, and turn from our wicked ways (see 2 Chronicles 7:14-15); that we would be fully obedient to God (see Deuteronomy 28:1-2); that our hearts would be fully committed to the Lord in obedience to His will (see 1 Kings 8:61); that we seek the things above, not the things of this earth (see Colossians 3:1-2); that we would become a new creation (see 2 Corinthians 5:17-18).

We now move to God's will for non-believers.

THE WILL OF GOD FOR NON-BELIEVERS

In addition, God's will for all people, including non-believers, is:

God's will is to reveal Himself to those who did not seek Him, *"I [God] revealed myself to those who did not ask for me; I was found by those who did not seek me. To a nation that did not call on my name, I said, 'Here am I, here am I'"* (Isaiah 65:1).

Those who seek God will find God. *"You will seek me [God] and find me when you seek me with all your heart"* (Jeremiah 29:13-14).

It is God's perfect patience that none should perish (see 2 Peter 3:9).

Next, we consider God's will for His church.

THE WILL OF GOD FOR HIS CHURCH

The church is to *"prepare God's people for works of service, so that the body of Christ may be built up until we all reach unity in the faith and in the knowledge of the Son of God and become mature, attaining to the whole measure of the fullness of Christ"* (Ephesians 4:12-13).

The church is to teach everyone in all wisdom, so that the person becomes mature in Christ. *"Him we proclaim, warning every man and teaching every man in all wisdom, that we may present every man mature in Christ (Colossians 1:28 RSV).*

The church is to be his witnesses; it is to make disciples; it is to worship Him; it is to honor the Son as the Head of the Body; it is to honor God's Word written; it is to be righteous; it is to feed the hungry; it is to heal the sick; it is to visit those in prisons; it is to be different than the world; it is to believe and accept God's promises; it is to follow God's commandments; it is to be the revelation of God.

Finally, we consider God's will for His creation.

THE WILL OF GOD FOR HIS CREATION

In order to express the will of God for His creation, let me say a word about creation. The word, *creation,* implies that it has no beginning, except through the will of God. Creation is the work of God in bringing into existence the universe, the heavens, and the earth, including both the material and the spiritual worlds. According to Scripture and the resulting Christian doctrine, God alone is eternal. Everything, physical and spiritual, was absolutely created, made out of nothing, by the power of the Almighty's Will. The first sentence of the Apostles' Creed is to be taken in its broadest and deepest sense, "I believe in God the Father Almighty, Maker of heaven and earth." The will of God for His creation is best captured by Paul in Romans 8:20-21, *"For the creation was subjected to frustration, not by its own choice, but by the will of the one who subjected it, in hope that the creation itself will be liberated from its bondage to decay and brought into the glorious freedom of the children of God" (Romans 8:20-21).*

Accordingly, God's will for His Creation is that it would be liberated from decay and renewed according to the initial purpose of God. So I conclude with this question. Why do we pray this petition, *Thy will be done in earth, as it is in heaven?*

There are several reasons why I believe we should pray this petition with conviction. God's will is all-encompassing and includes the very best for His creation. His will in heaven is dominated by love, righteousness, justice, and holiness. Why would we not want that condition here on earth?

I personally want, above all, His will for my life. I want to be obedient. Only then will I know the fullness of joy and peace and love. I want to tell others the good news of God. I want to know His love and His salvation. I want to be His witness. I want to be His minister for reconciliation. I want to tell the story of Jesus and His glory.

Discussion Questions

1. Why did Jesus come down from heaven (John 6:38-40)?

_____

_____

_____

_____

2. What is the Father's will for everyone (John 6:38-40)?

_____

_____

_____

_____

3. What is the reward for those who do the will of God (1 John 2:17)?

_____

_____

_____

_____

4. Who will equip you to do the will of God (Hebrews 13:20-21)?

_____

_____

_____

_____

5. What is the progressive change that God desires in His people?

_____

_____

_____

_____

6. What prevents us from knowing and doing the will of God (1 Corinthians 3:1-3)?

_____

_____

_____

_____

7. How would you describe/define the doctrine of reconciliation (Romans 5:11; 2 Corinthians 5:18-20)?

_____

_____

_____

_____

8. Why are God and man alienated?

_____

_____

_____

_____

9. How would you describe/define the doctrine of the Will of God?

_____

_____

_____

_____

10. What is the overall will of God?

_____

_____

_____

_____

11. What is the will of God for His Son?

_____

_____

_____

_____

12. What is the will of God for His Spirit?

_____

_____

_____

_____

13. What is the will of God for His saints?

_____

_____

_____

_____

14. What is the will of God for non-believers?

_____

_____

_____

_____

15. What is the will of God for His church?

_____

_____

_____

_____

16. What is the will of God for His creation?

_____

_____

_____

_____

17. Why do you pray this petition: _thy will be done on earth as it is in heaven_?

_____

_____

_____

_____

PETITION FOR PROVISION

CHAPTER 8

GIVE US THIS DAY OUR DAILY BREAD

HIS PROVISION

After this manner therefore pray ye: Our Father which art in heaven, Hallowed be thy name. Thy kingdom come. Thy will be done in earth, as it is in heaven. **Give us this day our daily bread.** *And forgive us our debts, as we forgive our debtors. And lead us not into temptation, but deliver us from evil: For thine is the kingdom, and the power, and the glory, forever. Amen.* (KJV)

Then the LORD said to Moses, "I will rain down bread from heaven for you. The people are to go out each day and gather enough for that day. In this way I will test them and see whether they will follow my instructions.

(Exod. 16:4)

Our forefathers ate the manna in the desert; as it is written: "He gave them bread from heaven to eat." Jesus said to them, "I tell you the truth, it is not Moses who has given you the bread from heaven, but it is my Father who gives you the true bread from heaven. For the bread of God is he who comes down from heaven and gives life to the world."

(John 6:31-33)

AFTER ADDRESSING THE person of God; we now study a series of petitions, the first of which is a request for the provision of God. The fundamental truth is that Jesus Christ is the bread of God and He gives life to the world (see John 6:31-33). Life is salvation, and salvation is through the bread of life.

It is sometimes dangerous to select a single passage for emphasis, but I believe that John 6:35 gives a unique insight into this petition, *give us this day our daily bread.*

Then Jesus declared, *"I am the bread of life. He who comes to me will never go hungry, and he who believes in me will never be thirsty."* Listen carefully. Jesus is talking about people coming to Him and believing in Him. The result will be that they will never hunger nor thirst. Keep that in mind as we examine this petition. Jesus is the bread of life; Jesus is the living water. Those who come to Him and believe in Him will never hunger nor thirst.

Jesus takes an Old Testament passage for this personal declaration. In Jeremiah, God said that He is the spring of living water: *"My people have committed two sins: They have forsaken me, the spring of living water, and have dug their own cisterns" (Jeremiah 2:13).* In the Old Testament, God is the spring of living water. This same thought is repeated at the end of the Bible, with Christ leading the redeemed to springs of living water. *"For the Lamb [Christ] at the center of the throne will be their shepherd; he [Christ] will lead them to springs of living water. And God will wipe away every tear from their eyes" (Revelation 7:17).* The spring of living water begins with God and continues with His Christ. God the Father and God the Son both provide food and drink for those who come to them and believe in them. In that regard, food and drink have both a physical and spiritual dimension.

With that brief introduction, we see that this petition is a request for *each day our daily bread,* but Scripture makes it clear that bread in divine terms can, and will be, both physical and spiritual. Above all, Scripture tells us the true bread is that which comes from God. This bread is Jesus Christ who came from heaven to give life to the world.

Now, praying this petition raises several interesting questions. Why do we ask for our daily bread each day? Most everyone is capable of getting bread for their needs. Many people might think,

I have been getting my own bread for years, all my life. Th
God didn't give me bread before I became a believer; God does...
need to give me bread now. I don't need God to give me each day
daily bread.

Many believers and unbelievers might think this very way. So
why does Jesus tell His disciples to go to God for their daily bread?
Why do we pray this petition? Well, when we pray these words,
Give us this day our daily bread, we are saying at least six things.
First, we are acknowledging our need for physical and spiritual
substances; second, the bread we are asking for is a special bread
that can come only from God; third, we are asking God for that
bread, which only He can supply; fourth, we are acknowledging
that His bread is the only one which can truly sustain, enrich, and
empower us; fifth, we are expressing our dependence on Him;
sixth, we are acknowledging our recognition of God as Jehovah
Jireh, our provider.

Now, the phrase itself, *Give us this day our daily bread*, has at
least three important messages.

First, this is a corporate prayer, give *us*. We are not just to
seek bread for ourselves, we are also to seek bread for our fellow
believers; second, Jesus instructs us to seek each day, the daily
provision of God; third, the daily bread we ask for is both physical
and spiritual.

So with this introduction, we will examine six issues: first,
the historical background of bread (manna); second, the concept
of this day our daily bread; third, the concept of daily bread as
contained in Scripture; fourth, Christ as the Bread of Life; fifth,
examples of bread as used in New Testament terms; sixth, why we
pray this petition.

THE HISTORICAL BACKGROUND OF *BREAD*

The history and nature of bread in the Bible provides an
interesting perspective to this petition. It essentially begins with
the history of Moses.

In Midian, God called Moses to go to Egypt and lead God's people out of bondage. The Israelites had physical needs and one of those was for physical *bread*. However, there was a great spiritual hunger that also needed to be met.

Then in the wilderness, the whole community grumbled against Moses and Aaron.

> *The Israelites said to them, "If only we had died by the LORD's hand in Egypt! There we sat around pots of meat and ate all the food we wanted, but you have brought us out into this desert to starve this entire assembly to death." Then the LORD said to Moses, "I will rain down bread from heaven for you. The people are to go out each day and gather enough for that day. In this way I will test them and see whether they will follow my instructions. On the sixth day they are to prepare what they bring in, and that is to be twice as much as they gather on the other days."*
>
> (Exod. 16:3-5)

God said, "*I will rain down bread from heaven*" (verse 4). This was to be a deluge, not a light sprinkling. And the purpose of God was to test them to "*see whether they will follow my [God's] instructions*" (verse 4).

Continuing in Exodus 16,

> *The LORD said to Moses, "I have heard the grumbling of the Israelites. Tell them, 'At twilight you will eat meat, and in the morning you will be filled with bread. Then you will know that I am the LORD your God.'" That evening quail came and covered the camp, and in the morning there was a layer of dew around the camp. When the dew was gone, thin flakes like frost on the ground appeared on the desert floor. When the Israelites saw it, they said to each other, "What is it?" For they did not know what it was. Moses said to them, "It is the bread the LORD has given you to eat. This is what the LORD has commanded: 'Each one is to gather as much as he needs. Take an omer for each person you have in your tent.'" The Israelites did as they were told; some gathered much, some little. And when they measured it by the omer, he who gathered much did not have too much, and he who gathered little did not have too little. Each one*

gathered as much as he needed. Then Moses said to them, "No one is to keep any of it until morning."

(Exod. 16:11-19)

This is the manna that God sent for His people then, and it is for daily bread that Jesus instructs us to pray today.

What is this *manna*, this daily bread? The Hebrew word, *manna*, is likely derived from the Egyptian word, *mennu*, food. The suggested source of the name is, "*They said one to another, 'what is it?'" i.e. manhu, which also means, "It is manna.*"

Manna becomes the great symbol of the providential care of God for the Israelites. The New Testament records that, inside the Holy of Holies in the temple, the ark of the covenant contained, among other things, the golden pot that had the manna (see Exodus 16:32-34; Hebrews 9:4). Moses commanded Aaron to put a pot of manna in the ark of the covenant (see Exodus 16:32-34), so future generations might see the bread of heaven on which their ancestors had fed.

The second issue is the uniqueness of this petition: *give us this day our daily bread.*

GIVE US THIS DAY OUR DAILY BREAD

In this prayer, we seek this day our daily provision from God. This is not something that we do occasionally. We are to turn to God each day asking for physical and spiritual sustenance. But why does Jesus tell us to ask *each day for our daily bread*? Why don't we ask for a weekly supply of bread? When we go to the store, we generally buy sufficient groceries to last a week or more. Jesus said that we are to pray each day for our daily bread, and not only that, He said we should ask God, our Father, to give us our *daily bread*, this day.

Why does Jesus say we should pray, *Give us this day our daily bread*? Why didn't Jesus just say: give us *this day* our bread? If not that, then why didn't Jesus just say, "Give us our *daily* bread?" In other words, "*this day*" and "*daily*" would seem on the surface to be redundant. Why did He say it this way? The reason is because there is a very important message here. We will find the answer as we look more closely at these two words, day and daily.

Now, the Hebrew and Greek words for daily add a significant dimension to our understanding of this petition. Our English words do not always mean what the Hebrew or Greek word would have meant. For example, the word, *daily*, more likely means *necessary*, or *the bread of our necessity*, or *what is necessary for us*. It can also be taken to mean that which is sufficient for our needs. Now the word, *day*, to the Israelites meant a specific time, generally as the period of time between two successive sunsets (see Genesis 1:5, 8; Leviticus 23:32).

As a result of this understanding, we are really praying, *Father, give us each day, bread sufficient and necessary for our sustenance.* We are not just asking for something each day, we are asking for something each day that will be *sufficient for our needs*. There is a great difference in praying the prayer in that light. We are asking for two things: first, day by day provision and, second, that the provision will be sufficient for our needs.

Jesus is reminding us of certain basic truths. First, in this prayer, we acknowledge that many times we cannot provide our daily bread for ourselves; second, we acknowledge that our Father is the One to whom we should turn for our daily bread; third, He is the only One who can meet our need for bread; fourth, we need to come to Him each day, not just once a week or whenever the cupboard is bare. We don't need to come to Him when we decide the time is right. We need to come to Him when He knows the time is right (which is each day) for our daily needs.

Now let us consider the possible place of Christ in this prayer. Here is the question: Is there any relationship at all to Jesus in this prayer? I think there is, as you shall see. Jesus had identified Himself as *the True Bread, the Living Bread, and the Bread of Life.*

CHRIST AS BREAD

In the Gospel of John (chapter 6), Jesus makes three important statements referring to Himself as *bread*.

First, Jesus said that He is the *True Bread* that came down from heaven. This phrase has an unusual meaning. *True* means that Jesus is the reality He appears to be, whose words and actions agree with His presence and that nothing is concealed. The Messiah stands before them and before us in this prayer. In addition, *true* always means that *truth* is the basis of all claims. It further means that He is superior to all, and everything else is inferior to Him.

"Jesus said to them, 'I tell you the truth, it is not Moses who has given you the bread from heaven, but it is my Father who gives you the true bread from heaven. For the bread of God is he who comes down from heaven and gives life to the world'"(John 6:32).

Second, Jesus said that He is the *Bread of Life.* *"Then Jesus declared, 'I am the bread of life. He who comes to me will never go hungry, and he who believes in me will never be thirsty'" (John 6:35).*

Jesus repeats this claim twice in 6:48. He is claiming that He is the bread that can give, sustain, and enrich life. In both passages, life has the meaning of salvation. Christ is the bread, which when eaten (received), brings salvation. *"I am the bread of life. Your forefathers ate the manna in the desert, yet they died. But here is the bread that comes down from heaven, which a man may eat and not die" (John 6:48-50).*

Third, Jesus said that He is the living bread. *"I am the living bread that came down from heaven. If anyone eats of this bread, he will live forever. This bread is my flesh, which I will give for the life of the world" (John 6:51).*

This reference is one of the most profound of all because the claim of living bread would directly connect Jesus as the Christ, the Messiah. This was one of the claims that the Jews expected from the Messiah. In the Midrash Koheleth, that commentary stated the following: "As was the first Redeemer, so shall be the latter. The first Redeemer [God] made manna descend from heaven (see Exodus 16:4); so also the later Redeemer [the Messiah] shall make manna descend." Jesus is moving far beyond any reference to bread; Jesus is now claiming that He is the Messiah, who has come down from heaven to reconcile the world to its Creator.

Christ continually refers to Himself as both the True Bread and the Living Bread from heaven who came so that we would have eternal life. The Living Bread is the Messiah. He is fulfilling all prophecy; He is the *bread* which defines Him as the Messiah.

When we pray for the daily bread, we are praying for both spiritual and physical needs, but above all, we are praying for the Son of God to fill us and nourish us with spiritual sustenance to fulfill God's purpose for our lives to advance the kingdom of God.

The Bible has several specific examples that further our understanding of the term, *bread.*

SPECIFIC EXAMPLES OF BREAD, AS USED IN SCRIPTURE

Now, to continue this story of manna and our daily bread, we find that there are many relevant events that shed considerable light on the matter of bread in general, as Christ as the true and living bread, and on this phrase, *"give us this day our daily bread."*

First, there is the confrontation of Jesus by Satan in a different wilderness. We are earlier reminded of the Exodus, but now the vision is that of the Christ, who would bring sinners out of a different slavery—from sin and into the marvelous light of His Father. The bondage to physical slavery in Egypt foreshadows the spiritual slavery to sin. *"Then Jesus was led by the Spirit into the desert to be tempted by the devil. After fasting forty days and forty nights, he was hungry. The tempter came to him and said, 'If you are the Son of God, tell these stones to become bread.' Jesus answered, 'It is written: "Man does not live on bread alone, but on every word that comes from the mouth of God"'"* (Matthew 4:1-4). In this confrontation, Jesus refers to Deuteronomy 8:3. By His sacrifice on the cross, Christ revealed His presence as the Bread of Life so that all people may receive forgiveness, redemption, reconciliation, and eternal life.

Second, there is the episode of the feeding of the 5,000. In this case, the prayer of Jesus led to the spiritual and physical multiplication of five loaves of bread and two fish to a meal for more than 5,000 men with their families. The Bread of God, Jesus Christ, provided for the physical needs of the people. This was the bread of God in action.

"'We have here only five loaves of bread and two fish,' they [the disciples] answered. 'Bring them here to me,' he [Jesus] said. And he directed the people to sit down on the grass. Taking the five loaves and the two fish and looking up to heaven, he gave thanks and broke the loaves. Then he gave them to the disciples, and the disciples gave them to the people. They all ate and were satisfied, and the disciples picked up twelve basketfuls of broken pieces that were left over. The number of those who ate was about five thousand men, besides women and children" (Matthew 14:17-21). Christ's actions here are a prelude to the institution of the Last Supper, the Eucharist. Again, at that time, Jesus Christ looked up to heaven, gave thanks, and broke the bread.

Third, there is the exchange in John's Gospel immediately following the feeding of the 5,000. Here Jesus relates manna in the wilderness to His earthly ministry.

"Our forefathers ate the manna in the desert; as it is written: 'He [God] gave them bread from heaven to eat.' Jesus said to them, "I tell you the truth, it is not Moses who has given you the bread from heaven, but it is my Father who gives you the true bread from heaven. For **the bread of God is he who comes down from heaven and gives life to the world.**" "Sir," they said, "**from now on give us this bread.**" Then Jesus declared, "I am the bread of life. He who comes to me will never go hungry, and he who believes in me will never be thirsty."

(John 6:31-35)

Notice that those who heard these words said to Jesus: "*From now on give us this bread.*"

He answered, "Your forefathers ate the manna in the desert, yet they died. But here is the bread that comes down from heaven, which a man may eat and not die. I am the living bread that came down from heaven. If anyone eats of this bread, he will live forever. This bread is my flesh, which I will give for the life of the world."

(John 6:49-51)

Fourth, there is the command of the Eucharist, regarding the body of Christ. Here Jesus Christ, the Living Bread, the Bread of God, the True Manna, is to be sacrificed for the sins of the world. Here the bread is symbolic of the body of Christ in the same way that the wine is symbolic of the blood of Christ. We celebrate His death in both thanksgiving and remembrance, until His coming again.

> While they were eating, Jesus took bread, gave thanks and broke it, and gave it to his disciples, saying, "Take and eat; this is my body." Then he took the cup, gave thanks and offered it to them, saying, "Drink from it, all of you. This is my blood of the [new] covenant [for the forgiveness of sins], which is poured out for many for the forgiveness of sins. I tell you, I will not drink of this fruit of the vine from now on until that day when I drink it anew with you in my Father's kingdom."
>
> (Matt. 26:26-29)

Paul also records the character of the Eucharist, in which he states that the bread is symbolic of the body of Christ.

> For I [Paul] received from the Lord what I also passed on to you: The Lord Jesus, on the night he was betrayed, took bread, and when he had given thanks, he broke it and said, "This is my body, which is [given] for you; do this in remembrance of me." In the same way, after supper he took the cup, saying, "This cup is the new covenant in my blood; do this, whenever you drink it, in remembrance of me." For whenever you eat this bread and drink this cup, you proclaim the Lord's death until he comes.
>
> (1 Cor. 11:23-26)

Fifth, John recorded the words of Jesus to the angel of the church at Pergamum. Jesus spoke of their sinful nature, but promised some of the hidden manna to those who overcome. "He who has an ear, let him hear what the Spirit says to the churches. To him who overcomes, I will give some of the hidden manna. I will also give him a white stone with a new name written on it, known only to him who receives it" (Revelation 2:17).

There is no doubt in my mind that Jesus had these events and passages in mind when He told His disciples to pray in this manner.

WHAT IS THIS DAILY BREAD THAT WE ARE TO PRAY FOR?

So what is this daily bread? The bread we pray for has both a physical and spiritual dimension. Is it truly physical bread, or do we seek that which bread represents? In truth, are we not asking God each day to meet our needs in a manner sufficient for the conditions in which we find ourselves? Our request is really for all that meets the physical and spiritual needs of life.

We are asking for two things: first, day-by-day provision and, second, that the provision will be sufficient for our needs.

WHY DO WE PRAY THIS PETITION: "GIVE US THIS DAY OUR DAILY BREAD"?

Many ask, "Can't we provide for ourselves? Do we need God for everything?" Yes, we do. However, praying this petition expresses our total dependence on *our Father*. Only God can fully satisfy our needs. Can we provide for ourselves better and more than God can do for us? I think not. God has the best and wants the best for His children. Do we want anything less than the best? Why would we settle for less than the best?

We pray this petition because we need God to meet our needs in a manner sufficient for the conditions of that day. Praying this petition, *give us this day our daily bread*, is an expression of love and confidence in our Father.

But, beyond provision, we also desperately seek pardon.

Discussion Questions

1. Why does God give the Israelites in the wilderness bread from heaven (Exodus 16:4)?

_____

_____

_____

2. What is the bread of God (John 6:30-34)?

_____

_____

_____

3. What is the result of the bread of God coming down from heaven?

_____

_____

_____

4. What do you learn/conclude from reading John 6:31-33?

_____

_____

_____

_____

5. What do you learn about "living water" as discussed in Jeremiah 2:13 and Revelation 7:17?

_____

_____

_____

_____

6. What truths do you learn from this passage, "Give us this day our daily bread"?

_____

_____

_____

_____

7. How would you describe the historical background of bread?

_____

_____

_____

_____

8. What is manna? What does the term mean?

_____

_____

_____

_____

9. What is the significance of the petition, "Give us this day our daily bread"? Why do we pray "this day" and "daily"?

_____

_____

_____

_____

10. How is Jesus Christ viewed as the Bread of God?

_____

_____

_____

11. Why is the term, Bread of God, so important as it relates to messianic prophecy?

_____

_____

_____

12. Give some examples of bread as used in events in Scripture.

_____

_____

_____

13. Why do you pray, "Give us this day our daily bread?"

_____

_____

_____

_____

PETITION FOR PARDON

CHAPTER 9

FORGIVE US OUR DEBTS

HIS PARDON

After this manner therefore pray ye: Our Father which art in heaven, Hallowed be thy name. Thy kingdom come. Thy will be done in earth, as it is in heaven. Give us this day our daily bread. And forgive us our debts, as we forgive our debtors. And lead us not into temptation, but deliver us from evil: For thine is the kingdom, and the power, and the glory, forever. Amen.

For if you forgive men when they sin against you, your heavenly Father will also forgive you. But if you do not forgive men their sins, your Father will not forgive your sins.

(Matt. 6:14-15)

Then Peter came to Jesus and asked, "Lord, how many times shall I forgive my brother when he sins against me? Up to seven times?" Jesus answered, "I tell you, not seven times, but seventy-seven times."

(Matt. 18:21-22)

If we confess our sins, he is faithful and just and will forgive us our sins and purify us from all unrighteousness.

(1 John 1:9-10)

THE BIBLE IS the rich story of the grace, mercy, and forgiveness of a loving, holy, righteous, and just God. It is also the story of the corruption, wickedness, evil, and sinfulness of mankind. It is about redemption, reconciliation, and renewed fellowship between God and mankind.

Our confession and our repentance of sin are the foundation for forgiveness and reconciliation. However, forgiveness is the unique quality of God, who seeks to redeem and justify (pardon and proclaim innocent) fallen mankind. The key to our forgiveness is that we are to forgive as we have been forgiven. Christians are part of a forgiving community; that is one of the blessings of our faith.

So Jesus, in this passage, tells us we should seek His pardon, but His pardon and His forgiveness are conditional. We ask, *Forgive us as we forgive others.*

This chapter addresses six themes: first, the matter of translations for the terms debts, trespasses, and sin; second, the nature of sin; third, the doctrine of divine forgiveness; fourth, the character of human forgiveness; fifth, the significance of this conditional phrase—*forgive us as we forgive*; sixth, the question of *why* we pray these words. Let us look at these six areas in order.

THE TRANSLATION OF THE TERMS: *DEBTS, TRESPASSES, AND SIN*

In this prayer, we ask that God will forgive us our debts, as we forgive our debtors. Some translations use the word *trespasses* or *sins* instead of the word *debts.*

In one way, this translation of debts and debtors raises many issues. A debt is normally money borrowed which one person is required by custom or law to pay back to another. In addition, almost all debts have some collateral associated with them. So, in this prayer, asking forgiveness for our debt implies that we have borrowed something from our Father and have given Him some collateral. Now we ask Him to forgive us of our debts, not hold our debts against us, and return all the collateral we have given Him. In that context, the word *debts* falls far short of that for which we seek forgiveness. We are not borrowers from God. God does not hold any collateral from us, and we are not asking Him to forgive our debts. No, the petition is far more important than that.

In fact, the word *debt* is used only seven times in the New Testament, five times by Jesus. All of these uses occur in the parable regarding the kingdom of heaven. It is interesting that Luke uses the word *sin* for debts in his version of the Lord's Prayer, recorded in Luke 11:1-4.

In certain other translations, the word *debt* is replaced by *trespasses*. Again that word falls short of what appears to be the intent of Jesus. Trespass is one form of sin, but it does not cover the subject adequately as we will shortly discuss. Trespass implies stepping over a boundary, and the boundary is one established by God. I believe that the proper term here is not debt or trespass, but *pure and unadulterated sin*. I have to believe that the request we make is: *Forgive us our sins as we forgive those who sin against us.*

Why do I believe that? But more importantly, what does the Bible teach? To begin with, the Bible makes it clear that man by nature is a sinner. As Scripture states: "*This righteousness from God comes through faith in Jesus Christ to all who believe. There is no difference, for all have sinned and fall short of the glory of God, and are justified freely by his grace through the redemption that came by Christ Jesus*" (Romans 3:22-25).

This passage states three truths: first, righteousness from God comes through faith in Jesus Christ; second, all of mankind has sinned and fall short of the glory of God; third, we are justified (pardoned, found innocent, and forgiven) by the grace of God.

The fate of all Christians is that of redeemed sinners, living in the midst of spiritual warfare. We are led by the Spirit and tempted by the devil. Victory over sin in our lives is the degree to which we accept the leading of the Spirit to resist the temptations of Satan.

To help us in spiritual warfare and to encourage us to refrain from sinning, the Father and the Son sent the Holy Spirit, so that we would understand the guilt of sin, the righteousness to which we are called, and the judgment that everyone shall face. Jesus stated this great truth in John 16:7: "*Unless I go away, the Counselor will not come to you; but if I go, I will send him to you. When he comes, he will convict the world of guilt in regard to sin and righteousness and judgment: in regard to sin, because men do not believe in me; in regard to righteousness, because I am going to the Father, where you can see me no longer; and in regard to judgment, because the prince of this world now stands condemned."*

Satan is the tempter, but God has given us the Spirit to guard and empower us. Jesus told us, *"When he [the Holy Spirit] comes, he will convict the world of guilt in regard to sin and righteousness and judgment: in regard to sin, because men do not believe in me [Christ]; in regard to righteousness, because I am going to the Father, where you can see me no longer; and in regard to judgment, because the prince of this world [Satan] now stands condemned"* (John 16:8-11).

Let me emphasize: the Spirit will convict the world of guilt with regard to sin, righteousness, and judgment. That is a powerful conviction, coming from the Spirit. However, the Spirit is also our guardian who not only leads us into all truth, but He indwells us to protect us against the temptations of Satan. Peter warns all disciples, *"Your enemy the devil prowls around like a roaring lion looking for someone to devour. Resist him, standing firm in the faith, because you know that your brothers throughout the world are undergoing the same kind of sufferings"* (1 Peter 5:8-9).

Satan tempts us to sin and encourages our continued life of sin. The temptations of life are great; however, we are called to resist the temptations. We are not to sin. We are not to yield to sin, but, if we do, we have an advocate with the Father, Jesus Christ, the righteous. The apostle John got it correct, *"My little children, I am writing this to you so that you may not sin; but if any one does sin, we have an advocate with the Father, Jesus Christ the righteous; and he is the expiation for our sins, and not for ours only but also for the sins of the whole world"* (1 John 2:1-2 RSV).

Although Christians are redeemed by grace through faith, sin and temptation always lie at the door. Paul states that the basis of salvation is through grace and our response in faith. *"For it is by grace you have been saved, through faith—and this not from yourselves, it is the gift of God—not by works, so that no one can boast. For we are*

God's workmanship, created in Christ Jesus to do good works, which God prepared in advance for us to do" (Ephesians 2:8-10).

Scripture emphasizes the word *sin* as indicative of that for which we seek forgiveness. We are sinners in need of forgiveness and redemption. However, we are also saints, which is the name reserved for those of faith in Christ Jesus, and who are the redeemed of the Lord. So I have to believe that the passage should more correctly read, *Forgive us our sins, as we forgive those who sin against us.*

In other words, Jesus came to take on our sins, not our debts, nor our trespasses. Listen to what the apostle John wrote. *"The next day John [the Baptist] saw Jesus coming toward him and said, 'Look, the Lamb of God, who takes away the sin of the world!'"* (John 1:29).

So we move to the second issue: What is this sin that Jesus takes away and what is this sin for which we seek forgiveness?

THE DEFINITION OF SIN

The underlying idea of sin is that of a Lawgiver, who is God, and His laws which He alone has written. As a result, sin is everything in the purpose and conduct of God's moral creatures that is contrary to God's expressed will, as contained in His laws (see Romans 3:20; 4:15; 7:7; James 4:12, 17). Another way of defining sin, based on biblical experience, is that sin is disobedience and/or transgression of the law of God.

However, sin is more than lawlessness: it is more than breaking a law. Sin is breaking a relationship, and the relationship being broken is the one we have with God. Sin is primarily an act, but there are thoughts and words that may well precede the act, and these thoughts and words can be just as sinful as the acts they represent. Jesus said that sin begins in the heart, even before the act is committed (The Sermon on the Mount). The sinfulness of sin lies in the fact that it is against God, even when the wrong we do is to others or ourselves (see Genesis 39:9; Psalm 51:4).

An exact definition of sin, based on biblical evidence, is that sin is the transgression of the law of God. *"Everyone who sins breaks the law; in fact, sin is lawlessness"* (1 John 3:4). It is that simple. As such, sin is rebellion, deliberate disobedience, failing to hit the target, and trespassing over a forbidden boundary. Sin is a violation of God's specific commandments. It is the act of an *enemy* of God. Sin deserves divine punishment because it is a violation of God's holy character (see Genesis 2:17; Romans 1:18-32; 1 Peter 1:16), but His pardon is gracious (see Psalm 130:4; Romans 5:6-8).

In order for God to forgive sin, two conditions are necessary. First, a life must be taken as a substitute for that of the sinner (see Leviticus 17:11, 14; Hebrews 9:22); second, the sinner must accept the sacrifice in a spirit of true repentance and true faith (Mark 1:4; Acts 10:43; James 5:15). Sin is evil at work in thought and/or in action. Unrighteousness or wickedness is the product of sin and the outward appearance of sin. And sin leads to spiritual death, which means eternal damnation and eternal separation from God.

Let me quote from the writings of Reverend Dr. Selwyn Hughes regarding the nature of sin. He discusses 1 John 1:6:

> People believe that they could live in fellowship with God and be unaffected and untouched in their daily lives and their relationships. The Gnostics alleged that they could live as they liked on the material level, providing they concentrated on developing the spiritual. John announced that morality is rooted in the nature of God, and that it is impossible to be in close relationship with Him without being moral. Morality is not merely God's will; it is God's nature. Many think that God arbitrarily decides certain things to be right and others to be wrong, and then issues commands accordingly. Nothing is further from the truth. God's laws are a transcript of His own character. We see revealed in Jesus a God who does everything He commands us to do. He obeys His own character, and does so because it is inherently right. This makes the universe of morality one and indivisible—for God and man. Sin then is serious to God, to the universe and to us. And morality is serious; serious to God, serious to the universe and serious to us. The way we act matters. It affects everything everywhere. The universe has a moral head, and a moral head after the pattern of the highest moral standard ever known—Jesus. To say that we have fellowship with Him and walk in darkness (moral disorder, sin) is to live a lie. And a lie, as someone said, has short legs—it

won't take you very far. Mark this: we cannot be in fellowship with God without being moral. Morality and spirituality are one. (Publication: *Every Day with Jesus—January 11, 2010*)

Paul stressed that sin came into the world through one man, Adam, and since then, all have sinned. *"Therefore, just as sin entered the world through one man [Adam], and death through sin, and in this way death came to all men, because all sinned—for before the law was given, sin was in the world"* (Romans 5:12-13). Paul further emphasized that *everything that does not come from faith is sin (see Romans 14:23).*

Paul also stated that Christ died for our sin, not for our debts. *"For what I received I passed on to you as of first importance: that Christ died for our sins according to the Scriptures, that he was buried, that he was raised on the third day according to the Scriptures, and that he appeared to Peter, and then to the Twelve"* (1 Corinthians 15:3-5).

God made him [Jesus Christ] who had no sin to be sin for us, so that in him we might become the righteousness of God. (2 Corinthians 5:21)

> *But the Scripture declares that the whole world is a prisoner of sin, so that what was promised, being given through faith in Jesus Christ, might be given to those who believe.*
>
> (Gal. 3:22)

> *But if we walk in the light, as he is in the light, we have fellowship with one another, and the blood of Jesus, his Son, purifies us from all sin.*
>
> (1 John 1:7)

But sin, confessed and repented, leads to forgiveness and reconciliation with God. So what is the divine forgiveness of God that we seek?

DIVINE FORGIVENESS

To understand divine forgiveness, we need to recall the text that contains the Jeremiah Covenant. *"Behold, the days are coming, says the LORD, when I will make a new covenant with the house of Israel and the house of Judah, not like the covenant which I made with their fathers when I took them by the hand to bring them out of the land of Egypt, my covenant which they broke, though I was their husband, says the LORD. But this is the covenant which I will make with the house of Israel after those days, says the LORD: I will put my law within them, and I will write it upon their hearts; and I will be their God, and they shall be my people. And no longer shall each man teach his neighbor and each his brother, saying, 'Know the LORD,' for they shall all know me, from the least of them to the greatest, says the LORD; for* **I will forgive their iniquity, and I will remember their sin no more"** *(Jeremiah 31:31-34 RSV).*

This covenant contains five eternal promises from God: first, I will put my law within them and I will write it upon their hearts. Second, I will be their God, and they shall be my people. Third, they shall all know me, from the least of them to the greatest. Fourth, I will forgive their iniquity. Fifth, I will remember their sin no more. In this covenant, God has promised to forgive our iniquity and to remember our sin no more.

This Jeremiah Covenant, this new covenant, for the forgiveness of sins, was ratified by the death of Christ on the cross. This is the forgiveness which God promises us in the Eucharist, our Communion service. *This is my body; this is my blood of the new covenant, which is poured out for many for the forgiveness of sins (see Matthew 26:26-29; Luke 22:17-20; 1 Corinthians 11:23-26).*

In this petition in The Lord's Prayer—*forgive us our sins as we forgive those who sin against us*—we seek forgiveness from God, but we acknowledge that His forgiveness is conditional on our forgiveness of others. We must understand that we are to forgive others in the same manner and to the same degree as God has forgiven us. We cannot expect forgiveness from God if we fail to forgive others.

God forgives. That is a fantastic statement. That is the promise contained in the Jeremiah Covenant. It is one of the great messages of Scripture, for the Bible is the only religious book that teaches that *God completely forgives sin* (see Psalm 51:1, 9; Isaiah 38:17; Hebrews 10:17).

God's unfailing love is contrasted with *my iniquity* and *my sin*. *"Have mercy on me, O God, according to your unfailing love; according to your great compassion blot out my transgressions. Wash away all my iniquity and cleanse me from my sin"* (Psalm 51:1-2). Isaiah 38:17 expresses confidence in the reconciling love of God that has kept the sinner from destruction. Through love, God does not see any of my sins. *"Surely it was for my benefit that I suffered such anguish. In your love you kept me from the pit of destruction; you have put all my sins behind your back"* (Isaiah 38:17).

Forgiveness is one of the great specialties of God. It is through His initiative (see John 3:16; Colossians 2:13) that He is ready to forgive. The great example is the story of the prodigal son (see Luke 15:11-32). Reading that story will provide an understanding of the way God forgives.

In addition, we have the witness of Scripture. *"For God so loved the world that he gave his one and only Son, that whoever believes in him shall not perish but have eternal life"* (John 3:16). God loved His creation. He didn't love without giving. He didn't give without loving. His love is so great that He wishes for us to spend eternity with Him.

> *When you were dead in your sins and in the uncircumcision of your sinful nature, God made you alive with Christ. He forgave us all our sins, having canceled the written code, with its regulations, that was against us and that stood opposed to us; he took it away, nailing it to the cross.*
>
> (Col. 2:13-14)

> *O LORD, we and our kings, our princes and our fathers are covered with shame because we have sinned against you. The Lord our God is merciful and forgiving, even though we have rebelled against him; we have not obeyed the LORD our God or kept the laws he gave us through his servants the prophets. All Israel has transgressed your law and turned away, refusing to obey you.*
>
> (Dan. 9:8-11)

God forgives because He is the God of grace, mercy, and pardon. Grace is giving us what we do not deserve, which is His love. Mercy is not giving us what we do deserve, which is His wrath. Pardon is our release from any punishment because God is ready to forgive (see Micah 7:18).

As I mentioned before, divine forgiveness required a tremendous price, because it is directly linked to the cross of Christ (see Acts 5:31; Colossians 1:14), His sacrificial death on the cross (see Romans 4:24-25), and His resurrection (see 2 Corinthians 5:15). God exalted Him to His own right hand as prince and savior that He might give repentance and forgiveness of sins to all people.

> *For he [God] has rescued us from the dominion of darkness and brought us into the kingdom of the Son he loves, in whom [Jesus Christ] we have redemption, the forgiveness of sins.*
>
> (Col. 1:13-14)

Since He bore the law's death penalty against sinners (see Galatians 3:10-13), those who trust in His sacrifice are freed from that penalty. By faith, sinners are justified and that carries the multiple character of being pardoned, declared innocent, and being forgiven (see Romans 3:28; Galatians 3:8-9).

Divine forgiveness is one of the most widely misunderstood doctrines of Scripture. It is not to be confused with human forgiveness that merely remits a penalty or charge. Divine forgiveness is one of the most complicated and costly undertakings, demanding complete satisfaction to meet the demands of God's love, justice, and holiness. Divine forgiveness demanded the cross.

We can never truly understand nor appreciate the price that the Son of God paid for the sins of the world. My sins and your sins put Christ on the cross. Redemption, restoration, and reconciliation are available because God Himself redeems His own. Such is divine forgiveness. Let us now compare divine forgiveness to human forgiveness.

Human Forgiveness

As expressed in this petition, we plead: *Forgive us as we forgive each other.* Therefore, human forgiveness must be part of our Christian makeup. However, human forgiveness is so much easier than divine forgiveness, and yet we find believers who cannot forgive themselves or others. However, the believer who belongs to this age is exhorted to be kind to believers and unbelievers, tenderhearted and forgiving to one another as God in Christ also has forgiven you (see Ephesians 4:32).

Christ taught that forgiveness is a responsibility for all Christians. Further, there are no limits to the extent of forgiveness (see Luke 17:4), and it must be granted without reservation. His answer to Peter was that one should forgive not merely seven times in a day, but seventy times seven (see Matthew 18:21-22). An unforgiving spirit is one of the offenses that God will not forgive (see Matthew 18:34-35). However, Christ also taught that there are conditions to be fulfilled before forgiveness can be granted. Forgiveness is one part of a mutual relationship. The other part is the confession and repentance of the offender. God does not, and cannot, forgive without genuine confession and genuine repentance. The effect of forgiveness is to restore to its former state the relationship that was broken by sin. Such a restoration requires the faith and trust of both parties. Confession and repentance must be sincere. If repentance is solely to escape any possible penalty or consequence, then there must be a question regarding the sincerity of the repentance. Confession and repentance are essential to the restoration of all human relationships.

Finally, Why Do We Pray: "*Forgive Us Our Sins as We Forgive Those Who Sin Against Us?*"

It is a simple recognition that I, like Paul, do not do the things that I want to do, but I do the things that I hate. I am in a constant state of needing divine and human forgiveness. I know that I shall not know divine peace until my sins are forgiven and I am reconciled to the fellowship of my Father who loves me so much as to send His Son to die for my sins. To obtain His forgiveness, I must be ready and willing to forgive those who have sinned against me. I accept that, and I desire to do that. I want to live in constant fellowship with my fellow man. I want to forgive myself and my fellows because that is the nature of God and I want His nature to be my nature. In one way, this is one of the paths to growing into the image of God.

Discussion Questions

1. What is the basis of God forgiving our sins?

_____

_____

_____

_____

2. How many times are we to forgive each other?

_____

_____

_____

3. What must we do to obtain forgiveness from God?

_____

_____

_____

4. What term should be used in this petition: debts, trespasses, sin, or any other? Why?

_____

_____

_____

5. What are three truths that you gather from Romans 3:22-25?

_____

_____

_____

_____

6. What is the fate of all Christians?

_____

_____

_____

7. What is the character of spiritual warfare (Ephesians 6:12-18)?

_____

_____

_____

8. What is the purpose/mission of the Spirit (John 16:7-11)?

_____

_____

_____

9. How must we treat Satan (1 Peter 5:8-9)?

_____

_____

_____

10. We are not to sin, but if we do, what can we look forward to (1 John 2:1-2)?

_____

_____

_____

_____

11. What is the nature of sin?

_____

_____

_____

_____

12. How would you define sin?

_____

_____

_____

_____

13. What is truly broken when we sin?

_____

_____

_____

_____

14. How would you describe divine forgiveness?

_____

_____

_____

_____

15. What is the price for us to receive divine forgiveness?

_____

_____

_____

_____

16. What does the cross teach us about sin?

_____

_____

_____

_____

17. What does "forgiveness" mean?

_____

_____

_____

_____

18. Why do you pray this petition: forgive us our sins as we forgive those who sin against us?

_____

_____

_____

_____

PETITION FOR PROTECTION

CHAPTER 10

AND LEAD US NOT INTO TEMPTATION

HIS PROTECTION-1

After this manner therefore pray ye: Our Father which art in heaven, Hallowed be thy name. Thy kingdom come. Thy will be done in earth, as it is in heaven. Give us this day our daily bread. And forgive us our debts, as we forgive our debtors. **And lead us not into temptation,** *but deliver us from evil: For thine is the kingdom, and the power, and the glory, forever. Amen.*

Then Jesus was led by the Spirit into the desert to be tempted by the devil.

(Matt. 4:1)

No temptation has seized you except what is common to man. And God is faithful; he will not let you be tempted beyond what you can bear. But when you are tempted, he [God] will also provide a way out so that you can stand up under it.

(1 Cor. 10:13)

When tempted, no one should say, "God is tempting me." For God cannot be tempted by evil, nor does he tempt anyone; but each one is tempted when, by his own evil desire, he is dragged away and enticed. Then, after **desire has conceived, it gives birth to sin; and sin, when it is full-grown, gives birth to death.**

(James 1:13-15)

125

*We know that the law is spiritual; but I am unspiritual, sold as a slave to sin. I do not understand what I do. For what **I want to do I do not do**, but what I hate I do....As it is, it is no longer I myself who do it, but it is sin living in me. I know that nothing good lives in me, that is, in my sinful nature. For I have the desire to do what is good, but I cannot carry it out. For what I do is not the good I want to do; no, the evil I do not want to do—this I keep on doing. Now if I do what I do not want to do, it is no longer I who do it, but it is sin living in me that does it.*

(Rom. 7:14-15, 17-20)

WE NOW ADDRESS the first of a two-part petition for divine protection which is vital to ensure our continued divine relationship with God in the face of temptations. The second part of this petition for protection (Chapter 11) will be dealt with in the next phrase, *but deliver us from evil.*

We know that temptation, not resisted, will lead to sin. Sin will lead to spiritual death, and spiritual death will lead to eternal separation from God. This phrase, *And lead us not into temptation,* might give the impression that, if we don't make this request, God is going to lead us into temptation. In other words, God might lead us into temptation if we don't ask Him not to. However, that is not the case at all. God does not tempt anyone (see James 1:13-15).

Satan is the tempter, and we are the ones who will be tempted and may be led into accepting and living the temptation. However, we will not be led by God; we will be led by Satan (James 1:13-15). Believers are like Jesus, *led by the Spirit...to be tempted by the devil.* That is the eternal state of all Christians. That is the challenge in this life which we must resist in order to live in the next.

It may also be the case that the more a person follows God and serves Him, the more likely Satan will attack that person. However, if you are not loving and serving God, Satan will probably ignore you. You are already separated from God. You've accomplished what he doesn't need to do. However, greater love and greater service to God may well bring greater temptations. Satan's ultimate goal is to separate believers from God, and he will use any device and any method he can to accomplish that.

So let's look more closely at temptation—its character, the different types, examples and warnings regarding temptation, and the solution for Christians when faced with temptation.

WHAT IS TEMPTATION?

Temptation is what makes the blood boil and the pulse rise. Many people might say, "You don't need to lead me into temptation. I can find it all by myself." And that is true. We can find temptation all by ourselves. Temptation is all around us. It wears many disguises. It is the lust of the eye, the lust of the flesh, and the pride of life.

However, temptation in Scripture does not always have a negative tone. Originally temptation had a neutral context, with the sense of testing a person's character or quality. For example, Abraham was tempted, or tested, when God told Abraham, "*Take your son, your only son Isaac, whom you love, and go to the land of Moriah. Sacrifice him there as a burnt offering on one of the mountains I will tell you about*" (Genesis 22:2). God put Abraham to the test. Abraham was faithful. Abraham passed the test.

Jesus was tempted to be a Messiah who could do spectacular things (see Matthew 4:1). Satan said, "'*All this [the kingdoms of the world] I will give you,*' he [Satan] said, '*if you will bow down and worship me*'" (Matthew 4:9). Jesus was tested (tempted), but Jesus said, "*Away from me, Satan! For it is written: 'Worship the Lord your God, and serve him only.' Then the devil left him, and angels came and attended him [Jesus]*" (Matthew 4:10-11).

There was evil implied in the temptations of Jesus. There is no evil implied in the temptation of Abraham. Therefore, temptation in Scripture has the possibility of holiness as well as the possibility of sin. While everyone experiences temptation, it is one thing to be tempted. It is another thing to fall. In one way, we are to rejoice in trials and temptation, for conquering temptation may lead to a higher, nobler, and more complete life.

Consider it pure joy, my brothers, whenever you face trials of many kinds, because you know that the testing of your faith develops

127

perseverance. Perseverance must finish its work so that you may be mature and complete, not lacking anything.

(James 1:2-4)

Temptation/testing can come from God or from Satan. If sent from God, we are to welcome the temptations that test our faith; if sent from Satan, we are to deny and turn from the temptations that lead to sin, spiritual death, destruction, and eternal damnation. The Lord's Prayer seeks that we may be spared from the testing of our faith which might lead us into evil acts.

WHAT ARE THE TYPES OF TEMPTATIONS?

Temptation generally occurs as the lust of the eye, the lust of the flesh, and the pride of life—these are the three great enemies of the Christian life.

Lust is an abnormal desire for that which is particularly forbidden by God. Therefore, lust refers to the desire for things that are contrary to the will of God. Lust can represent an abnormal sinful desire, not only for physical, but for spiritual satisfaction. The lust after evil things (see 1 Corinthians 10:6) of the Israelites in the wilderness serves as an example of the lusts that must be avoided by Christians. Lust includes the sinful desire known as fleshly and worldly, as opposed to spiritual and heavenly. Lust is the will of man as opposed to the will of God. It is generally evident in the sensual desire connected with adultery and fornication (see Matthew 5:28; Mark 4:19; John 8).

It is dangerous for a Christian to believe that lust includes only physical desires. When the will of man is contrary to the will of God, it takes on the guise of idolatry, which is going after other gods, worshiping other gods, and seeking satisfaction in this life for the things that are not of God.

Pride is also the great deceiver. What is pride and how do you recognize it? Pride is the evidence of insolence, arrogance, and an insulting nature leading many times to violence. It is being proud and boastful. It is about ourselves. Pride has nothing to do with God; in fact, pride separates us from God.

One of the central themes of the Old Testament is that God's judgment destroys all of man's pride. *"I [God] will punish the world for its evil, the wicked for their sins. I will put an end to the arrogance of the haughty and will humble the **pride of the ruthless**"* (Isaiah 13:11). Pride always ranks high in the catalogue of vices for pride is generally the result of idolatry.

> *Then your heart will become proud and you will forget the LORD your God, who brought you out of Egypt, out of the land of slavery.*
>
> (Deut. 8:14)

> *Love the LORD, all his saints! The LORD preserves the faithful, but the proud he pays back in full.*
>
> (Ps. 31:23)

> *The LORD detests all the proud of heart. Be sure of this: They will not go unpunished.*
>
> (Prov. 16:5)

Paul captures the full essence of pride in the catalogue of evil; here is what men of pride do.

> *They have become filled with every kind of wickedness, evil, greed and depravity. They are full of envy, murder, strife, deceit and malice. They are gossips, slanderers, God-haters, insolent, arrogant and boastful; they invent ways of doing evil; they disobey their parents; they are senseless, faithless, heartless, ruthless. Although they know God's righteous decree that those who do such things deserve death, they not only continue to do these very things but also approve of those who practice them.*
>
> (Rom. 1:29-32)

> *God opposes the proud but gives grace to the humble.*
>
> (James 4:6)

Pride is dangerous because it opposes God. The Bible says, *"God opposes the proud"* (1 Peter 5:5).

The Bible is filled with examples of temptation that serve as a warning to us. Let me identify a few.

EXAMPLES/WARNINGS OF TEMPTATION

One of the most telling and instructive passages regarding spiritual lust is in 1 Corinthians 10:1-13. Paul described the attitude of the Israelites in the wilderness and the displeasure of God with them. The Israelites committed both physical and spiritual lust. They tested God, and He was not pleased. Evil led to greater evil, and the lust of the spirit and the lust of the flesh dominated the people that God had called to be His witnesses to the world. Listen carefully to this story of the Israelites. We must not let this be the story for us or for our generation. The message in this passage is that constant reference to *as some of them were* or *as some of them did.*

> *For I do not want you to be ignorant of the fact, brothers, that our forefathers were all under the cloud and that they all passed through the sea. They were all baptized into Moses in the cloud and in the sea. They all ate the same spiritual food and drank the same spiritual drink; for they drank from the spiritual rock that accompanied them, and that rock was Christ. Nevertheless, God was not pleased with most of them; their bodies were scattered over the desert. Now these things occurred as examples to keep us from setting our hearts on evil things as they did. Do not be idolaters, as some of them were; as it is written: "The people sat down to eat and drink and got up to indulge in pagan revelry." We should not commit sexual immorality, as some of them did—and in one day twenty-three thousand of them died. We should not test the Lord, as some of them did—and were killed by snakes. And do not grumble, as some of them did—and were killed by the destroying angel. These things happened to them as examples and were written down as warnings for us, on whom the fulfillment of the ages has come. So, if you think you are standing firm, be careful that you don't fall! No temptation has seized you except what is common to man. And God is faithful; he will not let you be tempted beyond what you can bear. But when you are tempted, he will also provide a way out so that you can stand up under it.*
> (1 Cor. 10:1-13)

This passage is about four things: *as some of them did.* The four major sins were idolatry, sexual immorality, testing the Lord, and grumbling. Do we understand that grumbling is a sin ranking in the same category with idolatry? It is. Moreover, Paul writes that this experience in the wilderness was an *example,* and was written down as a *warning* for us. In truth, it is an example and a warning for all generations, including our own. We will be tempted, but we are not to do as the Israelites did in the wilderness. Their actions led to their condemnation. *God was not pleased with most of them.*

In the Sermon on the Mount, Jesus warned the world of the same problem. *"Do not be like them" (Matthew 6:8).* They do this; you are not to do that. Do not do as some of them did; do not be like them. Christians are constantly warned not to do as they did. Scripture is filled with this warning, and yet we continue to do the things that God said we should not do.

> They [Israelites] rejected his decrees and the covenant he [God] had made with their fathers and the warnings he had given them. They followed worthless idols and themselves became worthless. They imitated the nations around them although the LORD had ordered them, "Do not do as they do," and they did the things the LORD had forbidden them to do.
>
> (2 Kings 17:15)

When we follow worthless idols, we become worthless. Even worse than that, we become separated from God. What a condemnation!

> Again and again I [God] sent my servants the prophets, who said, "Do not do this detestable thing that I hate!" But they did not listen or pay attention; they did not turn from their wickedness or stop burning incense to other gods.
>
> (Jer. 44:4-6)

God sent His prophets, but they would not listen; they did not turn from idolatry. *"Why do you call me, 'Lord, Lord,' and do not do what I say?" (Luke 6:46).* This is a most condemning statement from Jesus. Don't call Jesus Lord [God] and not do what He says. Lip service is dangerous when dealing with the things of God.

> *We know that the law is spiritual; but I [Paul] am unspiritual, sold as a slave to sin. I do not understand what I do. For what I want to do I do not do, but what I hate I do.*
>
> (Rom. 7:14-15)

> *For the sinful nature desires what is contrary to the Spirit, and the Spirit what is contrary to the sinful nature. They are in conflict with each other, so that you do not do what you want.*
>
> (Gal. 5:17-18)

We will be tempted, and our faith will be tested. We will be *led by the Spirit...to be tempted by the devil.* As a result, many will do what they are told not to do. However, we must be faithful to God and do what He has commanded us to do.

We will face tests and temptations, and we must not try to avoid the test. Instead, we should welcome the challenge. However, we cannot face temptation on our own. God will equip us to pass the tests if we look to Him and do what is pleasing in His sight.

> *May the God of peace, who through the blood of the eternal covenant brought back from the dead our Lord Jesus, that great Shepherd of the sheep, equip you with everything good for doing his will, and may he work in us what is pleasing to him, through Jesus Christ, to whom be glory for ever and ever. Amen.*
>
> (Heb. 13:20-21)

WHAT IS THE SOLUTION FOR TEMPTATION?

So, as we reflect on this petition, one thing becomes clear. When tempted, God will *"provide a way out so that you can stand up under it"* (*1 Corinthians 10:13*). And that is why we pray, *Lord, lead me through the temptations of this world.*

Christians will be tested (tempted). However, praise God, there is an answer to both spiritual and physical lust. The Father and the Son have sent the Holy Spirit so that Christians are able to resist temptation. The flesh, with its passions and lusts, is to be crucified. Listen to the apostle Paul.

> So I [Paul] say, live by the Spirit, and you will not gratify the desires of the sinful nature. For the sinful nature desires what is contrary to the Spirit, and the Spirit what is contrary to the sinful nature. They are in conflict with each other, so that you do not do what you want. But if you are led by the Spirit, you are not under law.
> (Gal. 5:16-18)

The key, said Paul, is to live by the Spirit, and we will not give in to the desires of the sinful nature. The *acts of the sinful nature* are obvious: sexual immorality, impurity and debauchery, idolatry and witchcraft, hatred, discord, jealousy, fits of rage, selfish ambition, dissensions, factions and envy, drunkenness, orgies, and the like. Paul warns that those who live like this will not inherit the kingdom of God (see Galatians 5:19-21).

If we continue in our sinful nature, we will not inherit the kingdom of God. Look at the price that is to be paid for our sinful nature. We are to walk in the Spirit and exhibit the fruit of the Spirit.

> But the fruit of the Spirit is love, joy, peace, patience, kindness, goodness, faithfulness, gentleness and self-control. Against such things there is no law.
> (Gal. 5:22-23)

Instead, if we live by the Spirit (see Galatians 5:16), then we shall enjoy and display the fruit of the Spirit. Those who belong to Christ Jesus have crucified the sinful nature with its passions and desires. Since we live by the Spirit, let us keep in step with the Spirit. (see Galatians 5:16-25) Paul further states that we are to remember that we belong to Christ and we are to act as if we do.

Christians are to live by the Spirit. Is it easy to do? No. But if we empty ourselves and are filled with the Spirit, then we can begin to fulfill the promise of the image of God within us. The Spirit will lead us into all truth.

Paul advises us to put on the full armor of God. It is important if we are to resist temptation.

Finally, be strong in the Lord and in his mighty power. Put on the full armor of God so that you can take your stand against the devil's schemes. For our struggle is not against flesh and blood, but against the rulers, against the authorities, against the powers of this dark world and against the spiritual forces of evil in the heavenly realms. Therefore put on the full armor of God, so that when the day of evil comes, you may be able to stand your ground, and after you have done everything, to stand. Stand firm then, with the belt of truth buckled around your waist, with the breastplate of righteousness in place, and with your feet fitted with the readiness that comes from the gospel of peace. In addition to all this, take up the shield of faith, with which you can extinguish all the flaming arrows of the evil one. Take the helmet of salvation and the sword of the Spirit, which is the word of God. And pray in the Spirit on all occasions with all kinds of prayers and requests. With this in mind, be alert and always keep on praying for all the saints.

(Eph. 6:10-18)

Another significant way is to deny ourselves, take up our cross, and follow Jesus. Then Jesus said to his disciples, "*If anyone would come after me, he must deny himself and take up his cross and follow me*" *(Matthew 16:24).*

Mediating on these passages will equip the saints to resist the devil and the powers of this dark world and the spiritual forces of evil in the heavenly realms. Will we sin? Most likely. But the apostle John provides an answer for us. "*My little children, I am writing this to you so that you may not sin; but if any one does sin, we have an advocate with the Father, Jesus Christ the righteous; and he is the expiation for our sins, and not for ours only but also for the sins of the whole world*" *(1 John 2:1-2 RSV).* If we sin, we have an Advocate, Jesus Christ, the Righteous.

WHY DO WE PRAY: *LEAD US NOT INTO TEMPTATION?*

Lord, I pray this phrase because I want to do what you want me to do. I know that temptation will test me. I pray that I will pass the test. I do not want to sin because it can lead to spiritual death and eternal separation from God. I can't make it on my own.

There is a wonderful hymn: "*Turn your eyes upon Jesus; look full in His wonderful face. And the things of this world will grow strangely dim, in the light of His glory and grace.*"

Turn your eyes to Jesus. I pray to the Spirit of God: "*Lord, lead us through the temptations of life.*"

Discussion Questions

1. Describe what it means for you to hear that Christ was led by the Spirit to be tempted by the devil (Matthew 4:1)?

_____

_____

_____

_____

2. If you fall into temptation, what can you look forward to (1 Corinthians 10:13)?

_____

_____

_____

_____

3. How does Paul consider sin and temptation in his personal life (Romans 7:14-20)?

_____

_____

_____

_____

4. What is temptation?

_____

_____

_____

_____

5. What is the message of James considering temptation (James 1:2-4)?

_____

_____

_____

_____

6. What are different types of temptations?

_____

_____

_____

_____

7. Are there any that you associate with or have meaning to you especially?

_____

_____

_____

_____

8. What is lust?

_____

_____

_____

_____

9. What is pride?

_____

_____

10. How does God express His feeling regarding lust and pride?

11. What is the basic danger in pride?

12. What are some warnings and examples of temptation?

13. What is the solution for temptations in our lives?

14. What are the fruit of the Spirit (Galatians 5:22)?

_____

_____

_____

_____

15. To which ones do you relate? To which ones do you not relate?

_____

_____

_____

_____

16. Why do you pray: "Lead us not into temptation"?

_____

_____

_____

_____

CHAPTER 11

DELIVER US FROM THE EVIL ONE

HIS PROTECTION-2

*After this manner therefore pray ye: Our Father which art in heaven, Hallowed be thy name. Thy kingdom come. Thy will be done in earth, as it is in heaven. Give us this day our daily bread. And forgive us our debts, as we forgive our debtors. And lead us not into temptation, but **deliver us from evil**: For thine is the kingdom, and the power, and the glory, forever. Amen.*

*My prayer is not that you take them out of the world but that **you protect them from the evil one**.*

(John 17:15)

*Do not be afraid of what you are about to suffer. I tell you, the devil will put some of you in prison to test you, and you will suffer persecution for ten days. **Be faithful**, even to the point of death, and **I will give you the crown of life**.*

(Rev. 2:10)

And the devil, who deceived them, was thrown into the lake of burning sulfur, where the beast and the false prophet had been thrown. They will be tormented day and night forever and ever.

(Rev. 20:10.)

W E NOW COME to the second part of our petition for protection: *deliver us from evil.* In some translations, this passage reads: *deliver us from the evil one.*

Why did Jesus have this petition in this prayer? Why is it so important? Why do we ask for deliverance from evil and/or the evil one? These questions should be carefully considered. In general, we live in an evil environment, and one from which we pray to be delivered. As such, this leads to several theological subjects. First, what is this evil from which we seek protection? Second, who is Satan and what is the evil that he represents? Third, how are we delivered from the power of evil and the evil one? Fourth, why do I pray for this deliverance? Let's look at these four questions in order.

WHAT IS THIS EVIL FROM WHICH WE WANT DELIVERANCE?

Evil is a recognized spirit that opposes God and His work of righteousness in the world (see Romans 7:8-19). In Scripture, evil is a person's thoughts and actions that are contrary to the will and purpose of God. In general, evil can be either moral, intellectual, spiritual, physical, or a combination of all. The word, *evil,* is also used for any disturbance to the righteous, peaceful, and harmonious order of the universe.

Evil comes from Satan and him alone. He is the ultimate source of evil in the world; he is called the devil (see Luke 8:12) and the evil one (see Matthew 13:19). The Christian believer is assured that Jesus will triumph at the end of time, when Satan will be cast into a lake of fire and brimstone and evil will be overcome (see Revelation 20:10).

Evil also comes from the hearts of men (see Mark 7:20-23) who believe the lies of Satan, who accept the temptations of Satan, and who act in ways contrary to the will of God. Evil does not come from God, for God cannot be tempted by evil, nor does He tempt anyone (see James 1:13).

Evil is in the environment that surrounds us. We live in an evil world. We live among evil people who wish to do evil things to us and to others. Paul captured the essence of sin and evil in Romans 7:8-19:

But sin, seizing the opportunity afforded by the commandment, produced in me every kind of covetous desire. For apart from law, sin is dead. Once I was alive apart from law; but when the commandment came, sin sprang to life and I died. I found that the very commandment that was intended to bring life actually brought death. For sin, seizing the opportunity afforded by the commandment, deceived me, and through the commandment put me to death. So then, the law is holy, and the commandment is holy, righteous and good. Did that which is good, then, become death to me? By no means! But in order that sin might be recognized as sin, it produced death in me through what was good, so that through the commandment sin might become utterly sinful. We know that the law is spiritual; but I am unspiritual, sold as a slave to sin. I do not understand what I do. For what I want to do I do not do, but what I hate I do. And if I do what I do not want to do, I agree that the law is good. As it is, it is no longer I myself who do it, but it is sin living in me. I know that nothing good lives in me, that is, in my sinful nature. For I have the desire to do what is good, but I cannot carry it out. For what I do is not the good I want to do; no, the evil I do not want to do — this I keep on doing.

Paul is saying five things here. First, sin produces every kind of covetous desire; second, the idea of sin did not truly exist until the law defined the nature of sin; third, through the law, Paul recognized sin as sin; fourth, the law is spiritual, but Paul said we are unspiritual and slaves to sin; fifth, "*I [Paul] know that nothing good lives in me, that is, in my sinful nature. For I have the desire to do what is good, but I cannot carry it out*" (see Romans 7:19).

On our own, we are helpless to escape the power of evil. We desire to do good, but evil is at the doorstep, and we cannot do, in our own strength, what we know is right. If not restrained by the power of the Holy Spirit, we can be the victims of a sinful nature and a sinful world.

WHO IS SATAN AND WHAT IS THE EVIL THAT HE REPRESENTS?

Satan is a created, personal, evil representation of all that is opposed to God and men. The biblical perspective is that Satan, as the enemy of man, is primarily active in misleading and cursing humanity because of his intense hatred and opposition to God (see Matthew 13:39).

However, Christ redeems his people from him that had the power of death, that is, the devil (see Hebrews 2:14). Satan has the power of death, not as lord, but simply as executioner. As love, truth, and holiness characterize God, so malice or hatred (the spring of murder), lying, and uncleanness characterize Satan (see John 8:44; 1 John 3:10-12).

First, Satan tempts men to disbelieve in God. *"He [the serpent] said to the woman, 'Did God really say, "You must not eat from any tree in the garden"?'" (Genesis 3:1).*

Second, in the wilderness, Satan tempted Jesus, "If *you are the Son of God..." (Matthew 4:6).*

Satan is the epitome of pride and presumption (see Matthew 4:6). He also has restless energy, roaming about as a roaring lion, serpent, or dragon (see Job 1:7). He steals away the good seed from the careless hearer (see Matthew 13:19); he introduces the children of the wicked one into the church itself, the tares among which closely resemble outwardly the wheat (see Matthew 13:38-39). His power is that of darkness, from which Christ delivers His saints; cutting off members from Christ's church and delivering them to Satan (see 1 Corinthians 5:5; 1 Timothy 1:20; Acts 26:18). Satan's throne opposes Christ's heavenly throne (see Revelation 2:9-10, 13). He has his principalities and powers in his organized kingdom (see Romans 8:38; 1 Corinthians 15:24; Colossians 2:15; Ephesians 6:12). He instigates persecution and is the real persecutor. It is God's sole prerogative thoroughly to know evil without being polluted by it. That is the perspective that we should also have—to know evil and to recognize evil without being polluted by it.

The fundamental moral description of Satan is given by our Lord when He calls Satan the evil one (see Matthew 13:19, 38)—that is, the one whose nature and will are given to evil. Moral evil is his primary attribute. This description contrasts with the opposing and constant reference to God as the Holy One (see Isaiah 1:4).

The devil is the main title for the fallen angelic being who is the supreme enemy of God and man. Satan is his name, and the devil is what he is. He is the accuser or deceiver. He is also called the wicked or evil one (see Matthew 6:13; 13:19, 38; 1 John 2:13). These names depict the devil's fundamental nature. He is in direct opposition to everything God is or all God wishes to do. Satan is the source of all evil and wickedness. While the KJV reads, *Deliver us from evil,* the NKJV more accurately reads, *Deliver us from the evil one.* Humanity needs this deliverance, for the devil walks about like a roaring lion, seeking whom he may devour (see 1 Peter 5:8).

He is called the enemy (see Matthew 13:25, 28, 39); he is called the murderer (see John 8:44); he is called the deceiver (see Revelation 20:10); and he is called the prince of this world (see John 12:31; 14:30; 16:11). At Calvary, God dealt a deathblow to this world ruler. It is only a matter of time before God will win the final victory at the end of time (see 1 John 3:8; Matthew 25:41).

> *And there was war in heaven. Michael and his angels fought against the dragon, and the dragon and his angels fought back. But he was not strong enough, and they lost their place in heaven. The great dragon was hurled down — that ancient serpent called the devil, or Satan, who leads the whole world astray. He was hurled to the earth, and his angels with him.*
>
> (Rev. 12:7-9)

Satan is limited, judged, condemned, imprisoned, and has been reserved for judgment from the beginning. The outcome is certain though the process may be slow. The victory of Christ is the defeat of Satan.

> *Then a voice came from heaven, "I [God] have glorified it, and will glorify it again." The crowd that was there and heard it said it had thundered; others said an angel had spoken to him. Jesus said, "This voice was for your benefit, not mine. Now is the time for judgment on this world; now the prince of this world [Satan] will be driven out. But I, when I am lifted up from the earth, will*

draw all men to myself." He said this to show the kind of death he
was going to die.

(John 12:28-33)

I will not speak with you much longer, for the prince of this world
[Satan] is coming. He has no hold on me.

(John 14:30)

Revelation 12:9 verifies that, in connection with Christ's ascension, Satan was cast down to the earth and his angels with him. According to the passage immediately following (12:10-12), this casting down was not complete or final in the sense of extinguishing his activities altogether, but it involves the potential and certain triumph of God and His saints and the equally certain defeat of Satan. In Revelation 20, the future is confirmed that Satan will be bound a thousand years, then loosed for a little time, and then finally cast into the lake of fire.

Satan's plan is to separate us from God, to destroy the work of grace, and to disrupt all that would lead to the redemption and reconciliation of mankind with his Creator. The kingdom of darkness opposes the kingdom of light and would destroy the highest interest of God and mankind for the advancement of the kingdom of God and the salvation of mankind. Satan brings spiritual death; Christ has the power of spiritual life.

Truth is the foundation of the godly. Lies are the foundation of those who follow Satan. That is why Jesus proclaimed the reality of the truth. *"To the Jews who believed him, Jesus said, 'If you hold to my teaching, you are really my disciples. Then you will know the truth, and the truth will set you free'"* (John 8:31-32). This statement asserts that claiming and professing the truth is the only way of deliverance from the power of Satan.

HOW ARE WE TO BE DELIVERED FROM THE GRASP OF SATAN AND THE POWER OF SIN?

The devil is strong, but Christians are stronger through the Lord because we have the full armor of God.

146

Put on the full armor of God so that you can take your stand against the devil's schemes. For our struggle is not against flesh and blood, but against the rulers, against the authorities, against the powers of this dark world and against the spiritual forces of evil in the heavenly realms. Therefore put on the full armor of God, so that when the day of evil comes, you may be able to stand your ground, and after you have done everything, to stand.

(Eph. 6:11-13)

Christians have the protection needed to withstand his assaults. The devil tempts, but God provides a way of escape (see 1 Corinthians 10:13). The devil tries to take advantage of people (see 2 Corinthians 2:11), but Satan will flee if fought (see James 4:7). The devil should not be feared, for Jesus is more powerful than this deceiving prince of the demons.

You, dear children, are from God and have overcome them, because the one [Jesus Christ] who is in you is greater than the one [Satan] who is in the world.

(1 John 4:4)

The Christian knows that the triumph will be fulfilled at the end of the age, when Satan will be cast into a lake of fire and brimstone and evil will be overcome—and Jesus shall reign forever and ever. Amen.

Then I saw a great white throne and him [Christ] who was seated on it. Earth and sky fled from his presence, and there was no place for them. And I saw the dead, great and small, standing before the throne, and books were opened. Another book was opened, which is the book of life. The dead were judged according to what they had done as recorded in the books. The sea gave up the dead that were in it, and death and Hades gave up the dead that were in them, and each person was judged according to what he had done. Then death and Hades were thrown into the lake of fire. The lake of fire is the second death. If anyone's name was not found written in the book of life, he was thrown into the lake of fire.

(Rev. 20:11-15)

Paul closes chapter 7 of Romans with this thought: "*What a wretched man I am! Who will rescue me from this body of death? Thanks be to God — through Jesus Christ our Lord!*" (Romans 7:24-25).

The nature and the consequence of sin are that we are separated from God. So Paul wonders, as we all do: *Who will rescue us from the law of sin and death?* The answer: *Jesus Christ, our Lord. Thanks be to God.*

Who will restore and reconcile us to God? Jesus Christ, our Lord. Jesus Christ is the answer. Jesus Christ will rescue us from the law of sin and death. He will enable us to do the good we cannot do in our own strength and will. He is the basis of our redemption. He is the basis of our renewal. He is the basis of our reconciliation to God.

Rescued, redeemed, and reconciled, Paul now closes the argument with this great affirmation:

> *Therefore, there is now no condemnation for those who are in Christ Jesus, because through Christ Jesus the law of the Spirit of life set me free from the law of sin and death. For what the law was powerless to do in that it was weakened by the sinful nature, God did by sending his own Son in the likeness of sinful man to be a sin offering. And so he condemned sin in sinful man, in order that the righteous requirements of the law might be fully met in us, who do not live according to the sinful nature but according to the Spirit*
> (Rom. 8:1-4)

This message from the apostle Paul is clear and simple. We are free because God has set us free. In addition, God will graciously give us all things. Paul concludes this astounding truth and explanation of freedom from sin and death with the message that once we are Christ's, nothing can ever separate us from the love of God in Christ Jesus our Lord.

> *What, then, shall we say in response to this? If God is for us, who can be against us? He who did not spare his own Son, but gave him up for us all — how will he not also, along with him, graciously give us all things? Who will bring any charge against those whom*

God has chosen? It is God who justifies. Who is he that condemns? Christ Jesus, who died — more than that, who was raised to life — is at the right hand of God and is also interceding for us.

Who shall separate us from the love of Christ? Shall trouble or hardship or persecution or famine or nakedness or danger or sword? As it is written: "For your sake we face death all day long; we are considered as sheep to be slaughtered." No, in all these things we are more than conquerors through him who loved us. For I am convinced that neither death nor life, neither angels nor demons, neither the present nor the future, nor any powers, neither height nor depth, nor anything else in all creation, will be able to separate us from the love of God that is in Christ Jesus our Lord.

(Rom. 8:31-39)

WHY DO I PRAY "DELIVER US FROM EVIL"?

I have lived with evil all of my life. I have seen what evil can do to the hearts of people. I can see that evil will separate me from the love of God and from having a relationship with Him that is eternal. Evil is of this world. I want a world in which the will of God is known and expressed. I want a world in which the kingdom of God will come.

God is holy and righteous and just. He created me to be His child and live in His image. I want to be a child of God. I can only be that if, and when, I choose to follow Jesus Christ as my Savior and Lord. I want to be like Jesus. I want to have the mind of Jesus (see Philippians 2:5). I want to do what is right; I want to be a child of the King. Deliver me, O Lord, from the evil one.

Discussion Questions

1. Why do you pray for protection from the evil one (John 17:15)?

_____

_____

_____

_____

2. What is the primary function of Satan (Revelation 20:10)?

_____

_____

_____

_____

3. What is the character of evil (Romans 7:8-19)?

_____

_____

_____

_____

4. What is the source of evil in the world?

_____

_____

_____

_____

5. Who is exempt from the temptations of evil?

_____

_____

_____

_____

6. What is the essence of sin and evil (Romans 7:6-10)?

_____

_____

_____

7. What are five messages that Paul states in this passage?

_____

_____

_____

8. Who is Satan?

_____

_____

_____

9. What is the power that he represents?

_____

_____

_____

_____

10. Who can redeem us from Satan and the power of death?

_____

_____

_____

_____

11. What are various titles given to Satan?

_____

_____

_____

_____

12. Explain the final end of Satan as described in Revelation 12:7-9 and John 12:28-33.

_____

_____

_____

_____

13. How are we delivered from the grasp of Satan and the power of sin?

_____

_____

_____

_____

14. Discuss the great victory message of Romans 8:31-39. What are the major points and what is the single message that gives you hope and promise in an evil world?

_____

_____

_____

_____

15. Why do you pray: deliver us from the evil one?

_____

_____

_____

_____

THE PERSON OF GOD

CHAPTER 12

THINE IS THE KINGDOM, AND THE POWER, AND THE GLORY, FOREVER

After this manner therefore pray ye: Our Father which art in heaven, Hallowed be thy name. Thy kingdom come. Thy will be done in earth, as it is in heaven. Give us this day our daily bread. And forgive us our debts, as we forgive our debtors. And lead us not into temptation, but deliver us from evil: For **thine is the kingdom, and the power, and the glory, forever.** *Amen.*

But I [God] have raised you [Moses] up for this very purpose, that I might show you my power and that my name might be proclaimed in all the earth.

(Exod. 9:16)

At that time the sign of the Son of Man will appear in the sky, and all the nations of the earth will mourn. They will see the Son of Man coming on the clouds of the sky, with **power and great glory.** *And he will send his angels with a loud trumpet call, and they will gather his elect from the four winds, from one end of the heavens to the other.*

(Matt. 24:30-31)

And he [Jesus] said to them, "I tell you the truth, some who are standing here will not taste death before they see the kingdom of God come with power."

(Mark 9:1)

To him [Christ] who loves us and has freed us from our sins by his blood, and has made us to be a kingdom and priests to serve his God and Father — to him be glory and power forever and ever! Amen.

(Rev. 1:5-6)

All the angels were standing around the throne and around the elders and the four living creatures. They fell down on their faces before the throne and worshiped God, saying: "Amen! Praise and glory and wisdom and thanks and honor and power and strength be to our God forever and ever. Amen!"

(Rev. 7:11-12)

After this I heard what sounded like the roar of a great multitude in heaven shouting: "Hallelujah! Salvation and glory and power belong to our God, for true and just are his judgments."

(Rev. 19:1-2)

A S WE APPROACH the end of this prayer, I remind you that the first petition in this prayer was: *Thy kingdom come.* At the conclusion of this prayer, Jesus takes us back to the thought of the kingdom of God: *Thine is the kingdom, and the power, and the glory, forever.*

Jesus reminds us to conclude our prayer by focusing once more on God's kingdom, His glory, and His power. So let us examine this sentence that speaks of the divine kingdom, the divine power, and the divine glory. We must acknowledge that some texts omit this phrase. However, we shall examine that issue as we study the three terms. It is not certain whether this phrase was presented by Jesus at that time or was a later liturgical addition. However, the phrase is totally consistent with Scripture, and several Old Testament passages contain this same thought.

When King David spoke of the generosity of the people to build God's temple, his remarks contain this thought. *"Yours, O Lord, is the greatness and the power and the glory and the majesty and the splendor, for everything in heaven and earth is yours. Yours, O Lord, is the kingdom; you are exalted as head over all"* (1 Chronicles 29:11).

THINE IS THE KINGDOM, AND THE POWER, AND THE GLORY, FOREVER

The doxology by Peter also speaks to this phrase. *"So that in all things God may be praised through Jesus Christ. To him be the glory and the power for ever and ever. Amen"* (1 Peter 4:11).

If the phrase was not in the original, there seems to be sufficient precedence in Scripture for the idea expressed in it. We will never know for certain. However, I am prepared to welcome it as important, fitting, and appropriate. Let us now examine each element of this phrase.

THINE IS THE KINGDOM

The question is: why does Jesus have us return to the subject of the kingdom of God? The direct answer is that a principle emphasis of Jesus' earthly ministry was to proclaim the kingdom of God. Jesus began with that message. He ended with that message. The theme of the kingdom of God was basic to Him. He wants it to be basic for us.

Listen to these words. *"From that time on Jesus began to preach, 'Repent, for the kingdom of heaven is near"* (Matthew 4:17). Throughout The Gospel according to Matthew, the kingdom of God [heaven] is one of the central themes of that version of the Gospel. In addition, over half of the thirty-four parables in Matthew deal directly or indirectly with that subject. Jesus began His ministry directing our attention to the kingdom of God. He concludes the Gospel of Matthew by instructing His disciples to advance the kingdom by making disciples of all nations. He calls our attention to His perspective that the kingdom of God will include the disciples of all nations. *"All authority in heaven and on earth has been given to me. Therefore go and make disciples of all nations, baptizing them in the name of the Father and of the Son and of the Holy Spirit, and teaching them to obey everything I have commanded you. And surely I am with you always, to the very end of the age"* (Matthew 28:18-20).

In like manner, the Gospel according to Mark begins with this same emphasis on the kingdom of God. *"After John was put in prison, Jesus went into Galilee, proclaiming the good news of God. 'The time has come,' he said. 'The kingdom of God is near. Repent and believe the good news!'" (Mark 1:14-15)*. The Gospel according to Mark also concludes with the instruction to advance the kingdom of God. *"He [Jesus] said to them, 'Go into all the world and preach the good news to all creation'" (Mark 16:15)*. Mark reinforces the idea that the kingdom of God is to include *all creation*.

The Gospel according to Luke does not begin with that theme, but it closes with it. *"He [Jesus Christ] told them, 'This is what is written: The Christ will suffer and rise from the dead on the third day, and repentance and forgiveness of sins will be preached in his name to all nations, beginning at Jerusalem'" (Luke 24:46-48)*. As with Matthew and Mark, Luke also understands that the kingdom is inclusive, to all nations.

The Gospel according to John adds a special emphasis to the theme of the kingdom by declaring the importance of the new birth—a birth of the Spirit—as the essential means for *seeing* and *entering* the kingdom of God. In the discourse with Nicodemus, Jesus defined how a person must be born again. All of the gospel writers emphasized this truth. The kingdom of God is the essential message of the earthly teaching of Jesus. He is reminding us of that importance again in this acknowledgement in the Lord's Prayer. *Thine is the kingdom.*

THINE IS THE POWER

What is this power that is God? We are now addressing the character and attributes of God. We begin by understanding that God has both transferable and non-transferable attributes. His transferable attributes are: love, joy, peace, righteousness, holiness, and justice. His non-transferable attributes are His omnipotence, His omniscience, and His omnipresence. When we speak of man being in the image of God, we refer only to God's transferable attributes. Man will never be omnipotent, omnipresent, and omniscient. So when we speak of the *power* of God, we are referring to His omnipotence.

Omnipotence is an exclusive attribute of God and is consistent with the perfection of His being. It is consistent with His other two attributes, omniscience and omnipresence. By ascribing to God absolute power, we mean that He is able to do everything that is in harmony with His loving, wise, holy, and perfect nature.

> *One thing God has spoken, two things have I heard: that you, O God, are strong, and that you, O Lord, are loving. Surely you will reward each person according to what he has done.*
>
> (Ps. 62:11-12)

The eternal, infinite, and unlimited power of God is recorded in Scripture in connection with His work of creation (see Genesis 1:1; Romans 1:20); His redemption of mankind (see Luke 1:35,37; Ephesians 1:19); the conversion of sinners (see 1 Corinthians 2:5; 2 Corinthians 4:7); and the complete accomplishment of the great purpose of His kingdom (see Matthew 6:13; 13:31-32; 1 Peter 1:5; 1 Corinthians 15:1; Revelation 19:6). The only time the word "omnipotent" is used is in Revelation 19:6 (KJV and NKJV). In all other translations, the word used is *Almighty. The Lord God omnipotent reigneth* then is translated, *The Lord God Almighty reigns.* Whenever we see the word *Almighty,* we are to understand that it speaks of the omnipotence of God.

> *In the past God spoke to our forefathers through the prophets at many times and in various ways, but in these last days he has spoken to us by his Son, whom he appointed heir of all things, and through whom he made the universe. The Son is the radiance of God's glory and the exact representation of his being, sustaining all things by his powerful word.*
>
> (Heb. 1:1-3)

One of the invaluable references that sheds considerable light on this subject is the writing of James Orr in the *International Standard Bible Encyclopedia.* I quote:

> *"Power can be either divine or human. In both cases, power is indicative of might, strength, and force. If controlled properly, power can lead to acts of valor, rule, strength, might, and dominion. Power*

can be derived from many sources, (e.g. might, right, authority, and dictatorial control.) Generally, authority and power must be considered together. For example, authority is the basis of power; divine authority is the basis for divine power. However, right is also an equal basis of power. Might and dictatorial authority can also be the basis of power. All need to be considered. All have been evident in the world at one time or another."

The power that Jesus is describing in this prayer is the divine power derived from divine authority. That power is like the working of God's mighty strength, which He exerted in Christ when he raised him from the dead and seated him at his right hand in the heavenly realms, far above all rule and authority, power and dominion, and every title that can be given, not only in the present age but also in the one to come. *And God placed all things under his feet and appointed him to be head over everything for the church, which is his body, the fullness of him who fills everything in every way (see Ephesians 1:19-23).*

Jesus is the fullest and most complete expression of God's power. However, in the only passage where Jesus described Himself, He uses the word *gentle* as an expression of power. *"Take my yoke upon you and learn from me, for I am gentle and humble in heart, and you will find rest for your souls. For my yoke is easy and my burden is light" (Matthew 11:29-30).* In Jesus, gentleness is great divine power and omnipotence under perfect control. This is in opposition to violence that is great power out of control.

Throughout the Bible, God's power is recognized as unlimited and is attributed to Him and to Him alone. There are many passages that confirm the acknowledged power of God; let me list just four.

Yours, O Lord, is the greatness and the power and the glory and the majesty and the splendor, for everything in heaven and earth is yours. Yours, O Lord, is the kingdom; you are exalted as head over all.

(1 Chron. 29:11)

He [God] rules forever by his power, his eyes watch the nations — let not the rebellious rise up against him.

(Ps. 66:7)

To him who is able to keep you from falling and to present you before his glorious presence without fault and with great joy— to the only God our Savior be glory, majesty, power and authority, through Jesus Christ our Lord, before all ages, now and forevermore! Amen.

(Jude 24-25)

All the angels were standing around the throne and around the elders and the four living creatures. They fell down on their faces before the throne and worshiped God, saying: "Amen! Praise and glory and wisdom and thanks and honor and power and strength be to our God forever and ever. Amen!

(Rev. 7:11-12)

The full manifestation of God's power, as well as His love, is in the redemption and reconciliation of mankind to our Creator.

"Jews demand miraculous signs and Greeks look for wisdom. But we preach Christ crucified: a stumbling block to Jews and foolishness to Gentiles, but to those whom God has called, both Jews and Greeks, Christ the power of God and the wisdom of God. For the foolishness of God is wiser than man's wisdom, and the weakness of God is stronger than man's strength."

(1 Cor. 1:22-25)

At the end of the age, God's power will be fully evident in His reign and in His judgment.

And the twenty-four elders, who were seated on their thrones before God, fell on their faces and worshiped God, saying: "We give thanks to you, Lord God Almighty, the One who is and who was, because you have taken your great power and have begun to reign. The nations were angry; and your wrath has come. The time has come for judging the dead, and for rewarding your servants the prophets

163

and your saints and those who reverence your name, both small and great — and for destroying those who destroy the earth."

(Rev. 11:16-18)

We turn now to *thine is the glory.*

THINE IS THE GLORY

What is this glory that is unique to God alone? Glory conveys the ideas of beauty, majesty, and splendor. As such, glory is the possession and characteristic of Yahweh. It is inherent in His nature. It is to be recognized by His people and by everything that is associated with Him. Glory reflects His holiness, His righteousness, His justice, and His every act is a measure of His glory. To understand glory, a person has to understand love, holiness, righteousness, beauty, majesty, splendor, and every other attribute of God.

One of the fullest expressions of the glory of God was His *shekinah* glory during the Exodus and for years afterwards. This was God's visible manifestation in a cloud by day and the fire by night. It was His glorious light that led the Israelites from Egypt to the Promised Land. The word, *shekinah*, is often translated *to dwell in the midst of.* That is the sense in which it is used in Zechariah 2:10 and Haggai 1:8. The Old Testament implies that the *shekinah* glory of God was present down to the time of Nebuchadnezzar's destruction of the temple (see Joshua 3; 4; 6; Psalm 68:1; 132:8). *"By day, the Lord went ahead of them in a pillar of cloud to guide them on their way and by night in a pillar of fire to give them light, so that they could travel by day or night. Neither the pillar of cloud by day nor the pillar of fire by night left its place in front of the people"* (Exodus 13:21-22).

While Aaron was speaking to the whole Israelite community, they looked toward the desert, and there was the glory of the Lord appearing in the cloud (see Exodus 16:10).

God was evident in the pillar of cloud and the pillar of fire. Here the term "pillar" is used figuratively to describe the presence of God as He dwells in the midst of His people and holds everything together.

164

The New Testament retains this concept of the *shekinah* glory. However, the term used is more specifically as *the glory of the Lord*. Let us consider some New Testament passages regarding the glory of the Lord.

At the Incarnation:

*And there were shepherds living out in the fields nearby, keeping watch over their flocks at night. An angel of the Lord appeared to them, and the **glory of the Lord** shone around them, and they were terrified.*

(Luke 2:8-9)

The nature of the Son of God:

*The Word became flesh and made his dwelling among us. We have seen **his glory**, the glory of the One and Only, who came from the Father, full of grace and truth.*

(John 1:14)

The Heritage of the Jews:

*Theirs is the adoption as sons; **theirs the divine glory**, the covenants, the receiving of the law, the temple worship and the promises.*

(Rom. 9:4)

*For God, who said, "Let light shine out of darkness, made his light shine in our hearts to give us the light of the knowledge of **the glory of God in the face of Christ**."*

(2 Cor. 4:6)

To him who loves us and has freed us from our sins by his blood, and has made us to be a kingdom and priests to serve his God and Father — to him be glory and power forever and ever! Amen.

Look, he is coming with the clouds, and every eye will see him, even those who pierced him; and all the peoples of the earth will mourn because of him. So shall it be! Amen.

(Rev. 1:5-7)

I am frankly not sure that I can understand nor put into words the significance of what this means. I also am not sure that it is important to be able to state it in words—but I shall try. The problem is that we use these words, "glory," "majesty," "power," "beauty," and "splendor" differently today; but Scripture is the primary reference that should lead us to understand the beauty of God, the majesty of God and the splendor of God. *"Who among the gods is like you, O Lord? Who is like you—majestic in holiness, awesome in glory, working wonders?" (Exodus 15:11).*

Glory is the physical manifestation of the divine presence, but saying that does not do justice to His glory. For we immediately might ask the question: what is the physical manifestation of the divine presence? The best example I can find is that in Isaiah 6:1-10.

In the year that King Uzziah died, I saw the Lord seated on a throne, high and exalted, and the train of his robe filled the temple. Above him were seraphs, each with six wings: With two wings they covered their faces, with two they covered their feet, and with two they were flying. And they were calling to one another: "Holy, holy, holy is the Lord Almighty; the whole earth is full of his glory." At the sound of their voices the doorposts and thresholds shook and the temple was filled with smoke. "Woe to me!" I cried. "I am ruined! For I am a man of unclean lips, and I live among a people of unclean lips, and my eyes have seen the King, the Lord Almighty." Then one of the seraphs flew to me with a live coal in his hand, which he had taken with tongs from the altar. With it he touched my mouth and said, "See, this has touched your lips; your guilt is taken away and your sin atoned for." Then I heard the voice of the Lord saying, "Whom shall I send? And who will go for us?" And I said, "Here am I. Send me!" He said, "Go and tell this people: 'Be ever hearing, but never understanding; be ever seeing, but never perceiving.' Make the heart of this people calloused; make their ears dull and close their eyes. Otherwise they might see with their eyes, hear with their ears, understand with their hearts, and turn and be healed."

Isaiah was blessed to the see the Lord God, high and lifted up, and His train filled the temple. It is clear that Isaiah knew that it was God upon the throne by the shouts of the seraphs who exclaimed, *"Holy, holy, holy is the Lord Almighty; the whole earth is full of his glory."* Can we see that the whole earth is full of the glory of God? The Psalmists did; look at just two Psalms.

> *One thing I ask of the Lord, this is what I seek: that I may dwell in the house of the Lord all the days of my life, to gaze upon the beauty of the Lord and to seek him in his temple.*
>
> (Ps. 27:4)

> *For all the gods of the nations are idols, but the Lord made the heavens. Splendor and majesty are before him; strength and glory are in his sanctuary.*
>
> (Ps. 96:5-6)

That is the way I think we should look upon the Lord, our God. Beauty, splendor, and majesty are His. All we need to do is look around! Look around, that is all we shall see! So I conclude.

WHY DO I PRAY THIS PHRASE?

I do so because I mean it. *God, thine is the kingdom and the power and the glory forever.* There is no kingdom like God's kingdom; there is no power like God's power; there is no glory like God's glory. Clearly, it is all I want. I want to share the divine, as much as God will permit.

The summation of this is that great passage in Isaiah 52:7.

> *How beautiful on the mountains are the feet of those who bring good news, who proclaim peace, who bring good tidings, who proclaim salvation, who say to Zion, 'Your God reigns!*

> *Our God reigns! For thine is the kingdom and the power and the glory, forever and ever.*

Discussion Questions

1. Why did God call and anoint Moses (Exodus 9:16-17)?

2. What will the Second Coming of Christ be like (Matthew 24:30-31)?

3. What messages for today do you see in 1 Chronicles 29:11 and 1 Peter 4:11?

4. What was one of the principle messages of Jesus Christ regarding the kingdom of God?

5. To what extent is the kingdom of God a Jewish heritage or an all-inclusive heritage? Explain.

_____

_____

_____

_____

6. What is the power of God?

_____

_____

_____

7. What are two ways in which His presence and power are demonstrated?

_____

_____

_____

8. What are the ways in which God's power is evident?

_____

_____

_____

9. What does power indicate?

_____

_____

10. What divine power is derived from divine authority?

11. What is the most complete expression of God's power? Why?

12. What unique message do you see in Jude 24-25, regarding God's power?

13. What is the evidence of the full manifestation of God's power?

14. What is the glory that is unique to God alone?

_____

_____

_____

_____

15. Describe the shekinah glory of God, as revealed to the Israelites in the wilderness.

_____

_____

_____

_____

16. How is that shekinah glory demonstrated/understood in the New Testament?

_____

_____

_____

_____

17. How do you understand the glory of God?

_____

_____

_____

_____

18. Can you see the whole earth being filled by the glory of God? If so, how? If not, why not?

_____

_____

_____

_____

19. What is your personal feeling regarding Psalm 27:4? Do you seek the same thing that the Psalmist did?

_____

_____

_____

_____

20. Why do you pray: for thine is the kingdom and the power and the glory?

_____

_____

_____

_____

CHAPTER 13

AMEN

After this manner therefore pray ye: Our Father which art in heaven,
Hallowed be thy name. Thy kingdom come. Thy will be done in earth,
as it is in heaven. Give us this day our daily bread. And forgive us
our debts, as we forgive our debtors. And lead us not into temptation,
but deliver us from evil: For thine is the kingdom, and the power,
and the glory, forever. **Amen.**

I [God] said, "Obey me and do everything I command you, and you
will be my people, and I will be your God. Then I will fulfill the oath
I swore to your forefathers, to give them a land flowing with milk and
*honey — the land you possess today." I answered, "**Amen, Lord.**"*
(Jer. 11:4-5)

May the God of peace, who through the blood of the eternal covenant
brought back from the dead our Lord Jesus, that great Shepherd of
the sheep, equip you with everything good for doing his will, and
may he work in us what is pleasing to him, through Jesus Christ, to
whom be glory forever and ever. **Amen.**
(Heb. 13:20-21)

*To the angel of the church in Laodicea write: These are the **words of***
***the Amen,** the faithful and true witness, the ruler of God's creation.*
(Rev. 3:14-15)

THE WORD, *AMEN*, was first used in the Pentateuch in Numbers 5:22. As such, it became an important word in Jewish liturgy. Its use was continued by the first-century Christian assemblies. In the primitive Christian church, it was common for the people to say *Amen* at the close of a prayer.

The Hebrew word, *Amen*, means *firm, true, and faithful*. *"To the angel of the church in Laodicea write: These are the words of the Amen, the faithful and true witness, the ruler of God's creation"* (Revelation 3:14).

In Isaiah 65:16, the term, *The God of truth*, is a translation from the Hebrew which is really *The God of Amen*. *"Whoever invokes a blessing in the land will do so by the God of truth."*

The promises of God are Amen; that is they are true and faithful. For no matter how many promises God has made, they are *"Yes"* in Christ. *And so, through him, the "Amen" is spoken by us to the glory of God* (see 2 Corinthians 1:19-20).

Amen indicates united agreement in what is about to be said, or what had been said; therefore, it can be used at the beginning or end of a statement or a prayer. Used at the beginning of a sentence, it emphasizes what is about to be said. Used at the end of the statement or prayer, *amen* means, *I am in agreement. I acknowledge the truth of what I, or you, have just said.* It means the spoken truth, or what is spoken is faithful to the truth. Amen is also used as an adverb of assent or confirmation, *so let it be.*

Amen is the response of the hearers to the truth they have just heard or to the prayers that have been spoken. It is to affirm and confirm a prayer or a statement. By speaking the word, they made the substance of what was uttered their own.

A typical example is in Jeremiah 28:6, where the prophet endorses with *amen*, the words of the prophet Hananiah. He said, *"Amen! May the Lord do so! May the Lord fulfill the words you have prophesied by bringing the articles of the Lord's house and all the exiles back to this place from Babylon."*

As stated, the word is first used in Number 5:22. The last use of the word is in the last passage in the Bible, Revelation 22:20-21. *"He [Jesus Christ] who testifies to these things says, 'Yes, I am coming* soon.' *Amen. Come, Lord Jesus. The grace of the Lord Jesus be with God's people. Amen.*"

Notice that the last word in the Bible is *amen*. I am not sure, but its use in Revelation might possibly apply to the total agreement with the Word of God made flesh.

Amen is employed when an individual or the whole nation confirms a covenant or oath recited in their presence. It also occurs at the close of a psalm or book of psalms, or of a prayer.

Jewish tradition states that the people responded to the priest's prayer not with *amen*, but with, *Blessed be the name of the glory of His kingdom forever*. However, in synagogues, as in Christian assemblies, the response to prayers was *amen* (see 1 Corinthians 14:16).

A classic example of the use of the word is in Deuteronomy 27, where we see the word used as an expression of the agreement of the nation of Israel to the commands of God. Deuteronomy 27:9-14:

> *Then Moses and the priests, who are Levites, said to all Israel, "Be silent, O Israel, and listen! You have now become the people of the Lord your God. Obey the Lord your God and follow his commands and decrees that I give you today." On the same day Moses commanded the people: When you have crossed the Jordan, these tribes shall stand on Mount Gerizim to bless the people: Simeon, Levi, Judah, Issachar, Joseph and Benjamin. And these tribes shall stand on Mount Ebal to pronounce curses: Reuben, Gad, Asher, Zebulon, Dan and Naphtali. The Levites shall recite to all the people of Israel in a loud voice.*

The Levites then gave a series of commands and regulations to the people. After each command, Deuteronomy reported: "*Then all the people shall say, "Amen!"*

Examples of the use of *amen* in the Psalms include the following:

> *Praise be to the Lord, the God of Israel, from everlasting to everlasting. Amen and Amen.*
>
> (Ps. 41:13)

*Praise be to his glorious name forever; may the whole earth be filled
with his glory. Amen and Amen.*

(Ps. 72:19)

*Praise be to the Lord, the God of Israel, from everlasting to everlast-
ing. Let all the people say, "Amen!" Praise the Lord.*

(Ps. 106:48)

In the New Testament, Jesus used the companion term, *truly,
truly, I say to you. Amen, amen.* He introduced His declarations
with *Amen* in the beginning. In Matthew, Mark, and Luke, the
term is used singly, truly or verily, for *amen*. In John, the term is
always doubled: *verily, verily* for *amen, amen*. It is interesting that
the double amen is found twenty-five times at the beginning of
Jesus' major discourses. Paul used the term sixteen times in his
epistles. In each case, almost always, it is used as part of a doxology.
Finally, the apostle John recorded that *amen* is also a title for Christ.
Revelation 3:14. *"To the angel of the church in Laodicea write: 'These
are the words of the Amen, the faithful and true witness, the ruler of
God's creation.'"*

For me, the interesting point is that Jesus Christ identifies
Himself as the *Amen. This Amen—this Jesus*—is further identified
as the ruler of God's creation. I have to ask: does this mean that
God wants everything to be in agreement with His Son? I would
like to think that is true. It is the only explanation that I think is
accurate and consistent.

This identification of the *amen*, as the ruler of God's creation,
is totally consistent with Paul's statement in Colossians.

*He [Jesus Christ] is the image of the invisible God, the firstborn over
all creation. For by him all things were created: things in heaven
and on earth, visible and invisible, whether thrones or powers or
rulers or authorities; all things were created by him and for him.
He is before all things, and in him all things hold together. And
he is the head of the body, the church; he is the beginning and the
firstborn from among the dead, so that in everything he might have
the supremacy. For God was pleased to have all his fullness dwell*

in him, and through him to reconcile to himself all things, whether things on earth or things in heaven, by making peace through his blood, shed on the cross.

(Col. 1:15-20)

This is Jesus Christ, the great Amen.

In the Old Testament (see Isaiah 65:16), God is called the God of truth, because He remains eternally true. In the New Testament (see Revelation 3:14), Jesus Christ is given the same title for He too is eternally true and faithful.

Finally, it is interesting that several of the church Fathers refer to this custom of the people shouting *Amen.* Jerome said that at the conclusion of public prayer, the united voice of the people sounded like the fall of water or the noise of thunder. Would that it were so today!

And so we conclude our study and discovery of the great truths in The Lord's Prayer. Now let us step back and summarize where we have been.

Discussion Questions

1. What do you understand about the history and use of the term, *amen*?

_____

_____

_____

_____

2. What does the word mean?

_____

_____

_____

_____

3. To what term does the word, *amen,* relate?

_____

_____

_____

_____

4. What does the term indicate?

_____

_____

_____

_____

5. What is the last word in the Bible?

_____

_____

_____

_____

6. What, if anything, do you conclude from that?

_____

_____

_____

7. In Revelation 3:14-15, what do you learn about Jesus Christ?

_____

_____

_____

8. What does that title mean to you?

_____

_____

_____

9. What does it mean for God to be called the "God of truth"?

_____

_____

_____

CHAPTER 14

EPILOGUE
SUMMARY

After this manner therefore pray ye: Our Father which art in heaven, Hallowed be thy name. Thy kingdom come. Thy will be done in earth, as it is in heaven. Give us this day our daily bread. And forgive us our debts, as we forgive our debtors. And lead us not into temptation, but deliver us from evil: For thine is the kingdom, and the power, and the glory, forever. Amen.

And so we conclude. We began this journey with a discussion of the general characteristics of prayer, in which we concluded the following: one of the most meaningful measures of a relationship is conversation. The Bible defines prayer as conversation between God and man. Such divine conversation is an expression of our love for God because prayer can lead to a divine relationship. In this relationship, Christ is both our teacher and our example for a life of prayer. He teaches us that prayer is important because it unites us with our Father; prayer has power because the omnipotent God is involved. However, the proper attitude and spirit are essential for meaningful prayer. Further, Scripture witnesses to the importance of and power of prayer. Prayer is essential for a child of God to have a relationship with God, *our Father*.

We next examined The Lord's Prayer, to determine its overall characteristics. There appear to be at least three reasons why Jesus taught His disciples this prayer.

First, Jesus wanted us to understand, appreciate, honor, and love God as *Our Father.* Jesus proposes a new and closer relationship. God is enthroned in heaven, but also God has a far closer relationship with His adopted children. As Creator of all, Jesus now defined God as accessible to all. Since He is *Our Father,* then that defines us as "*His children.*" Defining God also defines us. "*What other nation is so great as to have their gods near them the way the Lord our God is near us whenever we pray to him?*" *(Deuteronomy 4:7).*

Second, Jesus knows that human beings have two fundamental needs: the physical and the spiritual. The spiritual can only be fully met by God, our Father.

Third, Scripture emphasizes that Jesus came to proclaim the kingdom of heaven. He wants us to emphasize the kingdom in our daily lives. He wants us to be kingdom-directed people.

Next, we sought to understand what it means to call *God Almighty, our Father.* The concept of the Fatherhood of God was one of the more important messages presented by Jesus during His earthly ministry. The idea of father is one of paternal love and care. The children are to honor the father, be obedient to the father, and they are to accept fully the authority of the father. These characteristics are true of earthly fathers. How much more is it the character and attribute of our heavenly Father!

God is to be honored, for He is the Father of the righteous, of kings, and priests, and prophets. If honor is due the earthly father, certainly God, as our heavenly Father, deserves and merits far more honor than that we would give to our earthly fathers. We are told that we all have one Father and our Father is in heaven.

*In the same way, let your light shine before men, that they may see your good deeds and praise **your Father in heaven.***

(Matt. 5:16)

182

*And do not call anyone on earth "father," for **you have one Father,
and he is in heaven.***

(Matt. 23:9)

There is yet another aspect of this relationship. God is not only our Father, but we, as His children, have a vision of the kingdom of God and we will share eternity in the kingdom of God.

Jesus answered him, "Truly, truly, [Amen, Amen] I say to you, unless one is born anew, he cannot see *the kingdom of God." Nicodemus said to him, "How can a man be born when he is old? Can he enter a second time into his mother's womb and be born?" Jesus answered, "Truly, truly, [Amen, Amen] I say to you, unless one is born of water and the Spirit, he cannot* enter *the kingdom of God."*

(John 3:3-5 RSV)

There is only one way that we can *see* and *enter* the kingdom of God. This can only happen by the new birth—the spiritual birth. We must be *born again* to be a child in God's kingdom. So Jesus says that when we pray, we begin by addressing God Almighty as our Father.

Next, we addressed the significance of the phrase, *who art in heaven.* In general, Scripture tells us that heaven is everything that has authority and power over man, gods, and spirits. In that sense, heaven became a general expression for everything that has positive and meaningful power and authority over man. Heaven means up; earth means down. Heaven conveys the thought of going up, such as climbing a mountain. It is up to the things of God and down to the things of man. But that is not to be the eternal condition.

With the symbolism of ascent and descent, up and down, there is the scriptural difference between above and below, between heaven as God's sphere and earth as man's. However, that is not necessarily an appropriate contrast because heaven and earth were both created by God and both are in God's sphere. Although earth may be more fully man's sphere, heaven definitely is not—in this age—in man's sphere. Therefore, we have the distinction between

183

a holy God and the sinful world. It is in this context that we can begin to understand the difference between heaven and earth. We discovered the biblical truth that there is no belief in heaven apart from belief in Jesus Christ. Such is the heaven for which we pray *Our Father, who art in heaven.*

When we pray *hallowed be thy name,* we understand that hallow represents the revealed nature of God. God has both a transferable nature and a non-transferable nature. When we grow into the image of God, we take on His transferable nature, which is His love, His righteousness, His patience, His joy, and His peace. These are characteristics that we are to seek and be evident in our lives. His non-transferable nature is His omnipotence, His omniscience, and His omnipresence; these are unique and are reserved for God alone. We, then, are to hallow both His transferable and non-transferable nature. In addition, God has several names that reflect both His character and His nature. Hear what the Word of God says, "*Do not profane my holy name. I must be acknowledged as holy by the Israelites*" (*Leviticus 22:32*).

The names of God reveal the character, purpose, and will of God. Sixteen names are used in the Old Testament to identify the Person of God. God has given Himself a name (Exodus 3:14-15), "*I AM WHO I AM.…this is my name forever, the name by which I am to be remembered from generation to generation.*"

So far, we have looked at three aspects of the Person of God. First, as "*Our Father,* second, *who art in heaven,* and third, *Hallowed be thy name.*

Next, we considered our first petition: *Thy kingdom come.* And what is this kingdom that we seek? In the most direct form, the kingdom of God is that moral and spiritual kingdom which the God of grace is establishing in this fallen world whose citizens willing accept His sovereign authority and power, and of which His Son Jesus is the glorified Head.

The presence of the kingdom of God in this world forever controls the course of human life and human history (see Matthew 13:24-33). Jesus explained how the wheat and the tares will be permitted to grow side by side, until the day of the harvest (the day of judgment), at which time the wheat (the righteous) and the tares (the evil) will be judged and forever separated. Only the wheat will know the fullness of eternal life with God. Further, the Son of God is the King of the kingdom. When the Son has accomplished His rule, then He will return the kingdom to the Father (see 1 Corinthians 15:23-28).

The purpose of the kingdom is the forgiveness, redemption, justification, propitiation, and reconciliation of all mankind and delivering them from the powers of evil (see 1 Corinthians 15:23-28).

The kingdom of God has at least six characteristics: it is an everlasting kingdom (see Daniel 7:27); it is a kingdom in which all the nations of the earth will be under the Lordship of God (see Isaiah 66:19-20); it is a kingdom which we must seek (see Matthew 6:33); it is a kingdom we must enter with childlike simplicity (see Mark 10:14-16); it is a kingdom not of this world. (see John 18:36); it is a kingdom in which only the *born again* can see and enter (see John 3:3-6).

Next, we examined the second petition, *thy will be done on earth as it is in heaven.* Here we address the doctrine of the will of God. We learned four things. First, we cannot understand the will of God until we have accepted Jesus Christ as Savior and Lord and been reconciled to our Father. We can't be reconciled unless we are in His will. His will is not known unless we are reconciled. Second, God will only reveal His will to His children, those who are *born again.* Third, reconciliation and the will of God are two closely interconnected doctrines. We must understand one to understand the other. Fourth, obeying His will leads to more complete reconciliation: being reconciled to God opens the window to understanding more fully His will. In the course of our examination, we recognize that God has a will for Himself, His Son, for His Spirit, for His saints, for His church, for unbelievers, and for His creation.

The Bible teaches that God and man are alienated from one another because of God's holiness and man's sinfulness. This contrast, between holiness and sinfulness, forces God to face a divine dilemma, which is: how does the holy God deal justly with sinful man? Although God loves the sinner (see Romans 5:8), it is impossible for Him to ignore sin (see Hebrews 10:26-27). Therefore, in biblical reconciliation, both parties are affected. Through the sacrifice of Christ, man's sin is atoned, and God's wrath is appeased. This is propitiation. Thus, a relationship of hostility and alienation is transformed into a relationship of love, unity, peace, and fellowship. That is the will of God that we want to be manifest on earth.

The next petition dealt with God's provision: *Give us this day our daily bread.* "*Then Jesus declared, 'I am the bread of life. He who comes to me will never go hungry, and he who believes in me will never be thirsty'*" *(John 6:35-36).* Jesus is talking about people coming to Him and believing in Him. The result will be that they will never hunger nor thirst. Jesus is the Bread of Life: Jesus is the Living Water. Those who come to Him and believe in Him will never hunger nor thirst.

God said that He is the spring of living water. "*My people have committed two sins: They have forsaken me, the spring of living water and have dug their own cisterns*" *(Jeremiah 2:13).* This Old Testament vision of God as the spring of living water is repeated at the end of the Bible, with Christ leading the redeemed to springs of living water. "*For the Lamb [Christ] at the center of the throne will be their shepherd; he [Christ] will lead them to **springs of living water**. And God will wipe away every tear from their eyes*" *(Revelation 7:17).* The spring of living water begins with God and continues with His Christ.

In the wilderness, the people complained to Moses and Aaron. In the desert, the whole community grumbled against Moses and Aaron. The Israelites said to them, "'*If only we had died by the LORD's hand in Egypt! There we sat around pots of meat and ate all the food we wanted, but you have brought us out into this desert to starve this entire assembly to death' Then the LORD said to Moses, 'I will rain down bread from heaven for you. The people are to go out each day and gather enough for that day. In this way I will test them and see whether they will follow my instructions'*" *(Exodus 16:3-4)*

God supplied bread from heaven. Jesus came to supply the same bread from heaven. He made three affirmations regarding bread. First, Jesus said that He is the True Bread that came down from heaven; this True Bread gives life to the world. (see John 6:32). Second, Jesus said that He is the Bread of Life (see John 6:35). Third, Jesus said, I am the Living Bread that came down from heaven (see John 6:51).

In this prayer, we are really praying, Father, give us each day, bread sufficient and necessary for our sustenance. We seek two things. First, day-by-day provision and, second that the provision will be sufficient for our needs. Praying this petition, *Give us this day our daily bread* is an expression of love and confidence in our Father.

Moving on, we next petition God to *forgive us our sins as we forgive those who sin against us.* Our prayer is a simple recognition that we, like Paul, do not do the things that we want, but we do the things that we hate (see Romans 7:15). Like Paul, we are in a constant state of needing divine and human forgiveness. We know that we shall not know divine peace until our sins are forgiven and we are reconciled and restored to the fellowship of our Father, who loves us so much, that He sent His Son to die for our sins. However, to obtain God's forgiveness, we must be ready and willing to forgive those who have sinned against us. In one way, seeking divine and human forgiveness is part of the path for growing into the image of God.

Next, we address the question of temptation and we pray to our Father, *lead us not into temptation.* To begin with, temptation in Scripture does not always have the negative tone of today. Originally temptation had a neutral context, with the sense of testing a person's character or quality. For example, Abraham was tempted, or tested, when God told Abraham to, *"Take your son, your only son Isaac, whom you love, and go to the land of Moriah, and offer him there as a burnt offering upon one of the mountains of which I shall tell you about" (Genesis 22:2-33).* God put Abraham to the test as a form of tempting. Abraham was faithful: Abraham passed the test.

James said that we are to rejoice when we face trials; we are to welcome the test. *"Consider it pure joy, my brothers, whenever you face trials of many kinds, because you know that the testing of your faith develops perseverance. Perseverance must finish its work so that you may be mature and complete, not lacking anything"* (James 1:2-4).

Temptation generally occurs in the lust of the eye, the lust of the flesh, and the pride of life—the three great enemies of the Christian life. Lust and pride can dominate many lives. Lust is basically an abnormal desire for that which is forbidden particularly by God. Pride is insolence, arrogance, insult, even violence. It is being proud and boastful. It is about ourselves. Pride has nothing to do with the things of God. *"God opposes the proud but gives grace to the humble"* (James 4:6). Pride is dangerous because it opposes God.

The apostle Paul said that the solution to temptation is to live by the Spirit and deny the desires of the sinful nature. *"So I [Paul] say, live by the Spirit, and you will not gratify the desires of the sinful nature. For the sinful nature desires what is contrary to the Spirit, and the Spirit what is contrary to the sinful nature. They are in conflict with each other, so that you do not do what you want. But if you are led by the Spirit, you are not under law"* (Galatians 5:16).

The second part of the protection that we seek is the petition, *deliver us from evil.* Evil is a recognized spirit that opposes God and His work of righteousness in the world (see Romans 7:8-19). Evil in Scripture is represented in any person or any act that is contrary to the will and purpose of God. Evil comes from Satan and from him alone. We are assured that Jesus will triumph at the end of the age when Satan will be cast into a lake of fire and brimstone and evil will be overcome (see Revelation 20:10). Evil does not come from God, for God cannot be tempted by evil, nor does He Himself tempt anyone (see James 1:13).

How will we be delivered from the evil that surrounds us?

Put on the full armor of God so that you can take your stand against the devil's schemes. For our struggle is not against flesh and blood, but against the rulers, against the authorities, against the powers of

*this dark world and against the spiritual forces of evil in the heavenly
realms. Therefore put on the full armor of God, so that when the day
of evil comes, you may be able to stand your ground, and after you
have done everything, to stand.*

(Eph. 6:11-14)

Who will deliver us from evil? Who will redeem us, reconcile
us, and restore us? Only Jesus Christ. He is our Redeemer.

Jesus now directs us back to the Father to remind us *For thine
is the kingdom and the power and the glory, forever and ever.* Jesus
wants us to recognize *"kingdom, power, and glory"* as eternal witnesses to God. Regarding the kingdom, Jesus begins and ends His
earthly ministry with emphasis on God's kingdom. As this theme,
the kingdom of God, was basic for Him, He wants it to be basic for
us. Jesus also calls us to acknowledge the power, the omnipotence,
of God. His omnipotence is exclusively an attribute of God and is
consistent with the perfection of His being. It is consistent with His
other two attributes: omniscience and omnipresence. By ascribing
to God absolute power, we mean that He is able to do everything
that is in harmony with His loving, wise, holy, and perfect nature.

Jesus next wants us to remember always the splendor and glory
of God. Glory conveys the ideas of beauty, majesty, and splendor. It
is inherent in His nature. It is to be recognized by His people and by
everything that is associated with Him. Glory reflects His holiness,
His righteousness, His justice, and His every act is a reflection of
His glory. To understand God's glory, we have to understand love,
holiness, righteousness, beauty, majesty, splendor, and every other
attribute of God. And Jesus tells us that the kingdom, the power,
and the glory are forever.

Jesus tells us to conclude this prayer with the word, *Amen,*
which means firm, true, and faithful. *"To the angel of the church
in Laodicea write: These are the words of the Amen, the faithful and
true witness, the ruler of God's creation" (Revelation 3:14).* In Isaiah
65:16, the term, *the God of truth* is a translation from the Hebrew
which is really *The God of Amen.* Whoever invokes a blessing in
the land will do so by the God of truth. The promises of God are
Amen; that is they are true and faithful.

189

In the Old Testament (see Isaiah 65:16), God is called the God of truth, because He remains eternally true. In the New Testament (see Revelation 3:14), Jesus Christ is given the same title for He too is eternally true and faithful.

It is interesting that several of the church fathers refer to this custom of the people shouting *amen,* and Jerome said that, at the conclusion of public prayer, the united voice of the people sounded like the fall of water or the noise of thunder. Again, would that it were so today!

Finally, I call your attention to the fact that the last word in the Bible is *Amen.* It may be speculation, but just maybe God is calling us to understand that we are to be in total agreement with the Word of God made flesh.

And so we conclude our study and discovery of the great truths in The Lord's Prayer. May God richly bless the reader and all who pray: *Our Father, who art in heaven.*

Discussion Questions

1. Why should prayer be considered a divine conversation?

_____

_____

_____

_____

2. Who is our teacher/example in prayer? Why?

_____

_____

_____

_____

3. What should be our proper attitude in prayer?

_____

_____

_____

_____

4. What should be our proper spirit in prayer?

_____

_____

_____

_____

5. What does it mean for you to call God, *Father*?

_____

6. What does it mean for God to be "in heaven"?

7. What does it mean to say: "hallowed be thy name"?

8. What is the kingdom of God?

9. What is the will of God for you?

10. Why do you pray: give us this day our daily bread?

_____

_____

_____

_____

11. What is the condition on which we pray that God would forgive our sins?

_____

_____

_____

_____

12. What is sin?

_____

_____

_____

_____

13. What are significant temptations that we all face?

_____

_____

_____

_____

14. Who is the Evil One?

_____

_____

_____

_____

15. What is his purpose?

_____

_____

_____

16. How is God's kingdom real in your life?

_____

_____

_____

17. What is God's power in your life?

_____

_____

_____

18. What is God's glory in your life?

_____

_____

_____

19. What have you learned about prayer in general?

_____

_____

_____

_____

20. Do you believe that your prayer life will be different/better?

_____

_____

_____

_____

21. What have you learned about The Lord's Prayer?

_____

_____

_____

_____

22. Why do you pray The Lord's Prayer?

_____

_____

_____

_____

BIBLIOGRAPHY

Brown, Colin, ed. *The New International Dictionary of New Testament Theology*. Grand Rapids, Michigan: Zondervan, 1971.

Elwell, Walter, ed. *Topical Analysis of the Bible*. Grand Rapids, Michigan: Baker Book House, 1972.

Hughes, Selwyn. *Every Day with Jesus*, Farnham, Surrey, UK: CWR Waverley Abbey House, 2010.

Jeremiah, David. *Prayer, The Great Adventure*. Colorado Springs, Colorado: Multnomah Books, 1997.

PC Study Bible formatted electronic database Copyright © 2003 Biblesoft, Inc. The following Bible Dictionaries are contained in this database: *Easton Bible Dictionary*, *Fausset's Bible Dictionary*, *Hitchcock's Bible Names Dictionary*, *International Standard Bible Encyclopedia*, *Nelson's Bible Dictionary*, *New Unger's Bible Dictionary*.

Stott, John R.W. *Basic Christianity*. Downers Grove, Illinois: Intervarsity Press, 1978.

Wetmore, William H. *God's Hidden Treasures*: The Parables of Jesus. Enumclaw, Washington: WinePress Publishing, 2002.

Wetmore, William H. *You Must be Born Again*. Enumclaw, Washington: WinePress Publishing, 2003.

Wetmore, William H. *Him We Proclaim*. Enumclaw, Washington: WinePress Publishing, 2002.

To order additional copies of this book call:
1-877-421-READ (7323)
or please visit our Web site at
www.WinePressbooks.com

If you enjoyed this quality custom-published book,

drop by our Web site for more books and information.

www.winepressgroup.com

"Your partner in custom publishing."

CPSIA information can be obtained at www.ICGtesting.com
Printed in the USA
LVOW05s1330130813

347677LV00003B/70/P